"Leeman airs the dirty laundry of our lives and talks about how to clean it up. He ventures into the tough area of pastoral application, which is sure to rouse good discussions, but again and again I found myself convinced. You will not fail to be helped by this book. Brief and biblical, wise and practical—this is the book on church discipline we've been looking for."

Mark Dever, Senior Pastor, Capitol Hill Baptist Church, Washington, DC

"Far too few biblically grounded, pastorally sensitive books on church discipline remain in print today. I know of none that is as exegetically accurate, practically relevant, and filled with real-life case studies of how churches should deal with a wide variety of common situations. On top of all this, Leeman is helpfully succinct and remarkably clear. Highly recommended!"

Craig Blomberg, Distinguished Professor of New Testament, Denver Seminary

"This book is an outstanding, one-of-a-kind theological work. Leeman has shown that church discipline is an essential dimension of the disciple-making process, and thus an extension of the preaching of the gospel itself. He shows that our overly-narrow focus on the 'number of decisions' might actually be hindering us from guiding people in the repentance that leads to life. I believe this will be the definitive work on church discipline, and our elders plan to use this work as our guide."

J. D. Greear, Lead Pastor, The Summit Church, Durham, North Carolina

"One of the most neglected activities in the church today is the ministry of loving, courageous, and redemptive church discipline. This book provides a clear vision and practical guidelines for this vital aspect of life together in the body of Christ. I have seen many people freed from entangling sin by churches that lived out these principles, and I pray that more and more churches will recommit themselves to this restorative ministry."

Ken Sande, President, Peacemaker Ministries

"Until such a time as the church of the Lord Jesus Christ becomes, by definition, a disciplined church, it will remain largely the undisciplined church. Leeman, of 9Marks, has provided another perceptive and important guide to establishing a healthy church through the exercise of unique Christian responsibilities, love, and discipline. The pastor with a desire to see a healthy church will profit immensely from this read."

Paige Patterson, President, Southwestern Baptist Theological Seminary

"Jonathan Leeman has become a discerning reader of the contemporary church. He combines biblical truth with sage counsel in this much-needed book on church discipline. If you've been afraid of that subject in your church, or unsure of how to lovingly correct sinning saints, this book provides the biblical argument and practical advice you need to get started well. This book will fire your imagination, stir your soul, and light your path."

Thabiti Anyabwile, Senior Pastor, First Baptist Church of Grand Cayman; author, *What Is a Healthy Church Member?*

"Many different ideas enter the minds of Christians when they hear the words 'church discipline'—punishment, judgment, critical, unloving, excommunication. Jonathan Leeman sets the record straight by explaining what Jesus meant when he first introduced this concept of spiritual accountability. Leeman explains the purpose of church discipline and why it is necessary. The case studies illustrating situations requiring church discipline are worth the price of the book!"

J. Carl Laney, Western Seminary; author, *A Guide to Church Discipline*

CHURCH DISCIPLINE

**Also available in the
9Marks Building Healthy Churches series:**

Edited by Mark Dever and Jonathan Leeman

Expositional Preaching: How We Speak God's Word Today,
   David Helm

*Sound Doctrine: How a Church Grows in the Love and Holiness
of God*, Bobby Jamieson

The Gospel: How the Church Portrays the Beauty of Christ,
   Ray Ortlund

Evangelism: How the Whole Church Speaks of Jesus,
   J. Mack Stiles

*Church Membership: How the World Knows Who Represents
Jesus*, Jonathan Leeman

Church Discipline: How the Church Protects the Name of Jesus,
   Jonathan Leeman

Discipling: How to Help Others Follow Jesus, Mark Dever

Church Elders: How to Shepherd God's People Like Jesus,
   Jeramie Rinne

BUILDING HEALTHY CHURCHES

CHURCH
DISCIPLINE

HOW
THE CHURCH
PROTECTS
THE NAME OF
JESUS

JONATHAN LEEMAN

WHEATON, ILLINOIS

Trade Paperback ISBN: 978-1-4335-3233-7
PDF ISBN: 978-1-4335-3234-4
Mobipocket ISBN: 978-1-4335-3235-1
ePub ISBN: 978-1-4335-3236-8

Library of Congress Cataloging-in-Publication Data
Leeman, Jonathan, 1973-
   Church discipline : how the church protects the name of Jesus / Jonathan Leeman.
      p. cm. — (9Marks : building healthy churches)
    Includes bibliographical references and index.
    ISBN 978-1-4335-3237-5 (hc)   ISBN 978-1-4335-3236-8 (epub)
    ISBN 978-1-4335-3234-4 (pdf)
    ISBN 978-1-4335-3235-1 (mobipocket)
    1. Church discipline. 2. Church discipline—Case studies. I. Title.
BV740.L44   2012
262'.8—dc22   2011043829

Crossway is a publishing ministry of Good News Publishers.

LB		23	22	21	20	19	18	17
14	13	12	11	10	9	8	7	6	5

CONTENTS

PART 3: GETTING STARTED

SERIES PREFACE

Do you believe it's your responsibility to help build a healthy church? If you are a Christian, we believe that it is.

Jesus commands you to make disciples (Matt. 28:18–20). Jude says to build yourselves up in the faith (Jude 20–21). Peter calls you to use your gifts to serve others (1 Pet. 4:10). Paul tells you to speak the truth in love so that your church will become mature (Eph. 4:13, 15). Do you see where we are getting this?

Whether you are a church member or leader, the Building Healthy Churches series of books aims to help you fulfill such biblical commands and so play your part in building a healthy church. Another way to say it might be, we hope these books will help you grow in loving your church like Jesus loves your church.

9Marks plans to produce a short, readable book on each of what we call the nine marks of a healthy church, plus one more on sound doctrine. Watch for books on expositional preaching, biblical theology, the gospel, conversion, evangelism, church membership, church discipline, discipleship and growth, and church leadership.

Local churches exist to display God's glory to the nations. We do that by fixing our eyes on the gospel of Jesus Christ, trusting him for salvation, and then loving one another with

God's own holiness, unity, and love. We pray the book you are holding will help.

With hope,
Mark Dever and Jonathan Leeman
Series editors

PREFACE

A Tale of Two Gospels

Which "gospel" do you believe in?

Your answer to that question will have a direct bearing on what you think about church discipline. Therefore, it's worth making sure we are talking about the same gospel before we talk about anything else.

Here are two subtly different versions of the gospel. The first one will probably shut down any talk about church discipline. The second one will start the conversation.

Gospel 1: God is holy. We have all sinned, separating us from God. But God sent his Son to die on the cross and rise again so that we might be forgiven. Everyone who believes in Jesus can have eternal life. We're not justified by works. We're justified by faith alone. The gospel therefore calls all people to "just believe!" An unconditionally loving God will take you as you are.

Gospel 2: God is holy. We have all sinned, separating us from God. But God sent his Son to die on the cross and rise again so that we might be forgiven and begin to follow the Son as King and Lord. Anyone who repents and believes can have eternal life, a life which begins today and stretches into eternity. We're not justified by works. We're justified by faith alone, but the faith which works is never alone. The gospel therefore calls all people to "repent and believe." A contraconditionally loving God will take you contrary to what you deserve, and then enable you by the power of the Spirit to become holy and obedient like his Son. By reconciling you to himself, God also reconciles you to his family, the church, and enables you as his people to represent together his own holy character and triune glory.

So what do you think? Which of these two gospels better characterizes what you believe the Bible teaches?

The first version emphasizes Christ as Savior. The second version emphasizes Christ as Savior and Lord.

The first version points to Christ's new covenant work of forgiveness. The second version includes both this and the Spirit's new covenant work of regeneration.

The first version points to the new status that Christians have as children of God. The second version includes both the new status and the new job description that Christians are given as citizens of Christ's kingdom.

The first version points to a Christian's reconciliation with Christ. The second version points to a Christian's reconciliation with Christ and Christ's people.

If your understanding of the gospel stops with the first version, you will not have much use for the topic of church discipline, or for this book. But if you embrace the second one, then there is a longer conversation to have. Aside from being an explicit biblical mandate, church discipline is an implication of the second version.

Everything affirmed in the first version is true, but there's more to say. Left to itself it tends to yield a belief in cheap grace. The second version, I believe, is a more robust account of the biblical gospel, and is more likely to lead to an understanding of the kind of grace that calls Christians to take up their crosses and follow Jesus in holy mission.

TWO RESPONSES TO CHURCH DISCIPLINE

My guess is that many church leaders over the last century would have affirmed the additional elements of gospel 2, at least if they were filling in test answer-sheet bubbles with a no. 2 pencil. But that's not what they have preached from the pulpit. It's not what they have said to Mr. and Mrs. Jones when they've brought six-year-old Johnny to their office and asked for him to be baptized.

Church leaders want to reach outsiders, but this good desire produces a bad temptation—to slim down the gospel to something skinnier. It's comparatively easy to talk about God's grace, unconditional love, and faith. It's harder to talk about God's holiness, Christ's lordship, a Spirit-given repentance, and the new covenant reality of the church. All of these things make demands on a person. They produce the need for accountability. And when you build a church on a gospel that makes few demands and offers little accountability, church discipline just doesn't make sense.

Picture a congregation that has been weaned on the spiritual milk of "just believe" and "unconditional love." Suppose you tell this congregation that it should consider excommunicating little Johnny because he is no longer six but twenty, and has not darkened the door of a church building since graduating from high school two years ago. Not only will you confuse that congregation, you will be running smack dab against its understanding of Christianity, like veering a car into oncoming traffic.

"You're judgmental."

"Why would an unconditionally loving God discipline anyone?"

"That sounds like legalism. We're saved by faith, not by works!"

"Once saved, always saved."

In other words, you will get run over.

But now picture a different congregation, one whose leaders have taught the members the gospel using the whole counsel of God. These members have been asked to count the cost of following Jesus from before they made professions of faith. They have heard that the kingdom of heaven belongs to the poor in Spirit, the pure in heart, the peacemakers (Matt. 5:4–9). They have heard that the heavenly Father will cut off every branch of Christ's vine that bears no fruit because the real gospel actually changes people (John 15:2). They have heard about the difference between worldly sorrow and godly sorrow: One looks like feeling sorry for yourself. The other looks like eagerness, indignation, fear, longing, and zeal (2 Cor. 7:10–11).

The second congregation is more likely to understand that God the Son really unites people to himself and to his family for life and growth. It will understand that God the Spirit really creates a whole new existence inside of people— that true Christians change. Tell these members that twenty-year-old Johnny has been absent for two years. They won't shrug their shoulders and sigh, "Once saved always saved," and get on with their work of singing praise songs. They will get on the phone and try to find Johnny, ask him for lunch plans, see how he's doing. They will call him to account for his claim to be a Christian. They might even, as a last-ditch effort to help him, excommunicate him. They love him too much not to. They love his non-Christian friends and colleagues too much not to.

SALT AND LIGHT

It is God's Word that gives life to the spiritually dead, but God means for his Word to be set against the backdrop of transformed lives. Transformed lives make a church's witness vivid and provocative. The world doesn't need a Christianized shadow of itself. It needs something full of light and flavor, something distinct.

> You are the salt of the earth, but if salt has lost its taste, how shall its saltiness be restored? It is no longer good for anything except to be thrown out and trampled under people's feet.
>
> You are the light of the world. A city set on a hill cannot be hidden. Nor do people light a lamp and put it under a basket, but on a stand, and it gives light to all in the house. In the same way, let your light shine before others, so that they may see your good works and give glory to your Father who is in heaven. (Matt. 5:13–16)

Salt is useful because it's distinct. Light is attractive to those standing in the dark because it's . . . not the dark.

INTRODUCTION

A Framework for Discipline

The main purpose of this book is not to persuade you about church discipline. It's to help the already-persuaded know how and when to practice it. Along these lines, it's important to see how the gospel of Jesus Christ gives us a theological framework for approaching church discipline. Church discipline, both formative and corrective, is an implication of the gospel. We will better understand how to approach it practically if we move *through the gospel* to get there.

That means my approach to the topic of church discipline is a little different than others have taken. Writers on church discipline from past centuries sometimes made lists from the Bible of which sins warrant church discipline. The idea was to give church leaders a basic guide for checking their own pastoral crises against.

Works on discipline from writers in our own day typically walk readers through the steps Jesus laid out in Matthew 18:15–20. They explain how to approach the sinner in private, then with two or three, then with the church. They pay less attention to different kinds of sin, and the widening-circle approach of Matthew 18 is treated as the catch-all.

There's much to commend both of these approaches, but

my method is a little different. I hope to establish a theological framework that accounts for the variety of approaches that the scriptural authors themselves take. For instance, Paul has a different approach in 1 Corinthians 5 than Jesus does in Matthew 18. Paul simply tells the church to exclude the sinner with no mention of first giving a warning. Why? Some writers have said that it's because the sin is "publicly scandalous." But that would seem to make the church's decision about who belongs to the kingdom of heaven depend on the evolving moral standards of society, which strikes me as strange. Is there not a theological connection between Matthew 18 and 1 Corinthians 5? I believe that there is, and we find it by considering church discipline in light of the gospel.

A theological-framework approach also helps leaders face up to the endless variety of circumstances and sins for which no exact scriptural case study exists—sins that don't show up on any list. If you have spent any amount of time as a pastor (or as a human), you know that sinners (like you and me) are endlessly creative. People don't always follow recipes when they cook up their sin; each pot of yuck is homemade and tastes a little different. My goal in part 1, therefore, is to establish a theological framework that helps church leaders approach the many different situations they find themselves facing.

TOUGH QUESTIONS

We at 9Marks receive a variety of church discipline questions from pastors seeking counsel. Here are a few that have recently rolled through my e-mail inbox:

- Can you discipline a nonmember?
- What should we do if one of our members completely abandons the faith and stops calling himself a Christian?
- Should a church accept the resignation of someone who is in unrepentant sin?
- After the church excommunicates someone, what should we do if another member refuses to disassociate from the excommunicated individual?
- Should we eat Thanksgiving dinner with a family member who has been disciplined?
- Does allowing a disciplined individual to continue attending church services eviscerate the act of discipline?
- What should we do about a longtime attending nonmember who's being divisive?
- What about a long-standing member who never attends and who's being divisive?
- Is pursuing marriage with a non-Christian a disciplinable offense?
- Is gluttony a disciplinable offense?
- Is anorexia or bulimia a disciplinable offense?
- Is believing the New Perspective on Paul a disciplinable offense?
- Are there different "levels" of discipline? Should a church respond to unrepentant adultery the same way it responds to habitual nonattendance?
- Should the church discipline teenage members who commit serious sin?
- At what point is it necessary to discipline a pastor? And who should lead that process?
- What are some specific guidelines for how church members should interact with a person who's been disciplined?
- With more serious and public sins, is it appropriate to

require someone to confess their sin before the whole church as proof of their repentance?

- When do we welcome an excommunicated individual back into fellowship? And how?

Getting a good theological framework in place helps to answer these questions, and more.

Admittedly, these questions are straightforward and limited in their scope. Real life often gets more difficult when you begin to peel back the multiple layers of sin and circumstance. What about the man who effectively cheats his clients out of their money without breaking any laws, goes bankrupt, gets sued by those clients, says he's repentant, but shows little interest in doing the difficult work of paying back those clients, since the money is gone and he doesn't want to spend the next ten years of his life making sacrifices?

What about the single mother of three children from three different men, all born out of wedlock, who is now pregnant with a fourth child from another man, and who breaks down in tears in the pastor's office? Does how hard she's crying tell you if she's really repentant?

What about the alcoholic who has several bad months, several good months, and then gets arrested on charges of public drunkenness? How much worse is the sin if there was an altercation with a police officer? Then again, what if this most recent incident was prompted by losing his job, or his wife separating from him? Should we be more lenient?

Here's a situation a church elder whom I've never met

asked me about on the telephone: a man's wife was unfaith-ful with another woman; he proceeded to divorce her even though she wanted the marriage to work; he then had several affairs of his own both before the divorce and after; and all of this was coming to light now, two years later, in the midst of the man's engagement to the senior pastor's daughter. What would you have said?

My best answer is often, "I have no idea, but I'll pray for you."

Beyond that, I use a theological framework for assessing a situation. My goal in part 1 of this book is to explain that framework to help you approach the variety of situations that arise in your church.

FUNDAMENTALIST RELIGION VS. GOSPEL WISDOM

So often in life it would be nice to have a rule book that made everything black and white: "When faced with *this*, do *that*." If you are a parent or a pastor, I expect you know exactly what I mean.

Knowing when and how to respond to the sin of fellow believers is the same way: "Can anyone tell me for certain whether now is the time to say something to Bob, or should I continue biting my tongue?"

Fundamentalist religion, in its more abrasive forms, seems to be motivated by this desire for clarity. It wants black-and-whites in places where the Bible is silent. It demands certainty where none is offered.

Why would God ever leave things unclear? My guess is that, among other things, he means for us to cry out for wisdom, because crying out for wisdom requires naturally self-sufficient people like us to lean on him. All those gray areas in life function as training grounds for trust.

That said, God's Word does provide us with the broad guidelines, or framework. Our task is to understand that framework and then sensitively apply it from one situation to another, always walking in trust, always asking for wisdom. That's what part 2 of this book represents. It's not a fundamentalist's book of case law: "When faced with *this*, do *that*." Rather, it's my attempt to demonstrate how the basic framework might apply in various kinds of scenarios so that you get a better idea of what the process looks like. The decisions made do not represent the "final word." They represent my or other pastors' best attempts at applying gospel wisdom. They also allow me to use more situational nuance than the principle-establishing chapters in part 1 allow for.

As with several of the illustrations above, I have created these "case studies" using elements out of real life situations I have been involved with or at least heard about. In all of them, I have altered the details in various ways.

Part 3 rounds out the book by offering advice on leading your church toward practicing formal church discipline: what do you need to teach your congregation and what structures do you need to get in place.

SHOULD WE PRACTICE DISCIPLINE?
Should your church practice church discipline? Yes. First of all, church discipline is loving. It shows

- love for the individual, that he or she might be warned and brought to repentance;
- love for the church, that weaker sheep might be protected;
- love for the watching world, that it might see Christ's transforming power;
- love for Christ, that churches might uphold his holy name and obey him.

By abstaining from discipline, on the other hand, we claim that we love better than God loves. God, after all, "disciplines those he loves," and "he punishes everyone he accepts as a son" (Heb. 12:6, NIV).

He knows that discipline yields life, growth, and health: "God disciplines us for our good, that we may share in his holiness" (Heb. 12:10, NIV).

Yes, it's painful, but it pays off: "No discipline seems pleasant at the time, but painful. Later on, however, it produces a harvest of righteousness and peace for those who have been trained by it" (Heb. 12:11, NIV). Can you see the rolling fields of righteousness and peace? That's the promise God gives us.

So love should motivate all of a church's discipline. Do you love? Then discipline. Discipline is not a word the culture understands, and the movement from love to discipline is certainly not something the culture understands. But this is what the Bible teaches. Do you think it's true?

More concretely, churches should practice discipline because

- it's biblical;
- it's an implication of the gospel;
- it promotes the health of the church;

- it clarifies and burnishes the church's witness before the nations;
- it warns sinners of an even greater judgment to come;
- (most importantly) it protects the name and reputation of Jesus Christ on earth.

Jesus has attached his name to the church. He has staked his reputation on us. Strange, isn't it? Now, the whole matter does not finally rest on our shoulders. He has proven through the life of Old Testament Israel that he will do whatever it takes to protect his name. Still, he gives our churches a job to do: to care for his name and reputation before the nations. Like it or not, the world will draw its conclusions about him based on us.

Church discipline, fundamentally, is about making sure that Jesus's representatives on earth represent Jesus and not someone else.

If you need more persuasion to practice discipline in your church, I recommend chapter 7 of Mark Dever's *Nine Marks of a Healthy Church*. Other good books on the topic include *The Transforming Community* by Mark Lauterbach, *Walking Together* by Wyman Richardson, *Love that Rescues* by Eric Bargerhuff, and Jay Adam's now classic *Handbook of Church Discipline*. You'll also find a number of shorter articles at www.9Marks.org.

I also hope the overall framework of the following few chapters is persuasive. It should point to a picture of Jesus's people learning to look like Jesus, precisely so that the nations would marvel.

24

Part 1

ESTABLISHING A FRAMEWORK

1

THE BIBLICAL BASICS
OF DISCIPLINE

What is church discipline? In broad terms, church discipline is one part of the discipleship process, the part where we correct sin and point the disciple toward the better path. To be *discipled* is, among other things, to be *disciplined*. And a Christian is disciplined through instruction and correction, as in a math class where the teacher teaches the lesson and then corrects the students' errors.

It's for this reason that there's a centuries-old practice of referring to both formative discipline and corrective discipline. Formative discipline helps to form the disciple through instruction. Corrective discipline helps to correct the disciple through correcting sin. This book focuses on corrective discipline, but teaching and correction always work together. That's the nature of discipleship.

In more specific and formal terms, church discipline is the act of removing an individual from membership in the church and participation in the Lord's Table. It's not an act of forbidding an individual from attending the church's public gatherings. It is the church's public statement that it can no longer affirm the person's profession of faith by calling him or her a Christian. It's a refusal to give a person the Lord's Supper. It's excommunicating, or ex-communion-ing, the person.

To be clear, then, I will treat these terms synonymously: "to excommunicate" is "to exclude from fellowship," which is to "remove from the Lord's Table," which is "to formally discipline." Some people treat one or two of these things as different stages in the process; I do not.

JESUS ON DISCIPLINE

Many texts in the New Testament point to the practice of church discipline. The most well known is probably from Matthew's Gospel. Jesus says,

> If your brother sins against you, go and show him his fault, just between the two of you. If he listens to you, you have won your brother over. But if he will not listen, take one or two others along, so that "every matter may be established by the testimony of two or three witnesses." If he refuses to listen to them, tell it to the church; and if he refuses to listen even to the church, treat him as you would a pagan or a tax collector. (Matt. 18:15–17, NIV)

On the surface, Jesus appears to have two concerns: first, that the sinner repents; second, that the number of people involved remain as small as necessary for producing repentance. Beneath these concerns is the deeper conviction that the church should look different than the world—Christians are not to live like pagans or tax collectors. Matthew's Jewish audience would have understood "pagan" to represent those who were outside the covenant community and "tax collector" to represent those who had betrayed the covenant community (and were therefore also outside the community). Church members should live differently than the world. And if, after a series of gracious warnings, they don't, a church should exclude them from its fellowship.

The sin described here is an interpersonal one: "against you." Yet I believe we often overemphasize the significance of this detail. The issue here is whether the individual is repentant and to be treated as a brother or sister in Christ. The larger point in these verses is that local churches have the authority to assess professions of faith and to act accordingly: "if two of you agree on earth about anything they ask" (Matt. 18:19). In other words, churches can employ the process of church discipline described in verses 15 to 17 to sins more broadly.

In short, Jesus means for churches to play a judicial function. He draws the language about "two or three witnesses" from Deuteronomy 19, a passage where Moses laid out rules of procedure for judging criminal cases. When faced with people who claim to represent Jesus with their lips but who live contrariwise, churches must carefully weigh the evidence and render judgment. "Is this a valid gospel profession? Is this a true gospel professor? What does the evidence suggest?"

THE APOSTLES ON DISCIPLINE

The apostle Paul also invokes church discipline in a number of places:

> Brothers, if anyone is caught in any transgression, you who are spiritual should restore him in a spirit of gentleness. (Gal. 6:1)

> Take no part in the unfruitful works of darkness, but instead expose them. (Eph. 5:11)

> Warn a divisive person once, and then warn him a second time. After that, have nothing to do with him. (Titus 3:10, NIV)

> If anyone does not obey what we say in this letter, take note of that person, and have nothing to do with him, that he may be ashamed. Do not regard him as an enemy, but warn him as a brother. (2 Thess. 3:14–15)

John encourages something like preemptive discipline by not letting someone participate in the fellowship of the church in the first place:

> Everyone who goes on ahead and does not abide in the teaching of Christ, does not have God. Whoever abides in the teaching has both the Father and the Son. If anyone comes to you and does not bring this teaching, do not receive him into your house or give him any greeting. (2 John 9–10)

Peter also presents us with a clear example of preemptive discipline (Acts 8:17–24).

DISCIPLINE IN CORINTH

One last famous passage on church discipline is 1 Corinthians 5. Paul lays out the sin and his reaction to it in the first few verses of the chapter:

> It is actually reported that there is sexual immorality among you, and of a kind that is not tolerated even among pagans, for a man has his father's wife. And you are arrogant! Ought you not rather to mourn? Let him who has done this be removed from among you.
>
> For though absent in body, I am present in spirit; and as if present, I have already pronounced judgment on the one who did such a thing. (1 Cor. 5:1–3)

What's striking about Paul's counsel is how it both overlaps and does not overlap with Jesus's counsel in Matthew 18. Like Jesus, Paul encourages the church to play a judicial function. He even uses the words "judgment" or "judge" several times (1 Cor. 5:3, 12–13). Like Jesus, Paul is addressing a scenario where someone professing the name of Jesus could be removed from the church body. Unlike Jesus, however, Paul does not tell the church to warn the man and call him to repentance, like Jesus advises in Matthew 18. He simply tells the church to remove him—no questions asked. We'll discuss the rationale for this in chapter 3.

In the ensuing verses, Paul more carefully describes what this act of discipline should look like:

> When you are assembled in the name of the Lord Jesus and my spirit is present, with the power of our Lord Jesus, you are to deliver this man to Satan for the destruction of the flesh, so that his spirit may be saved in the day of the Lord. (1 Cor. 5:4–5)

To hand the man over to Satan is to treat him, in Jesus's words, like a pagan or tax collector; it's to treat him as someone who no longer belongs to the covenant community.

The church, after all, is an outpost of the kingdom of God. Everyone who does not belong to the kingdom of God, therefore, belongs to the kingdom of Satan. Satan is the prince of this world, and the kingdoms of the world temporarily belong to him (John 12:31; 14:30; Matt. 4:8–9).

Paul next observes that failing to remove the man from the church puts the whole church at risk:

> Your boasting is not good. Do you not know that a little leaven leavens the whole lump? Cleanse out the old leaven that you may be a new lump, as you really are unleavened. For Christ, our Passover lamb, has been sacrificed. Let us therefore celebrate the festival, not with the old leaven, the leaven of malice and evil, but with the unleavened bread of sincerity and truth.
>
> I wrote to you in my letter not to associate with sexually immoral people—not at all meaning the sexually immoral of this world, or the greedy and swindlers, or idolaters, since then you would need to go out of the world. But now I am writing to you not to associate with anyone who bears the name of brother if he is guilty of sexual immorality or greed, or is an idolater, reviler, drunkard, or swindler—not even to eat with such a one. (1 Cor. 5:6–11)

In the final verses of the chapter, Paul reiterates the fact that the church has a judicial role to play in this man's life: "For what have I to do with judging outsiders? Is it not those inside the church whom you are to judge? God judges those outside. 'Purge the evil person from among you'" (vv. 12–13).

THE PURPOSE OF CHURCH DISCIPLINE

First Corinthians 5 is especially helpful for discerning the purposes of church discipline. We can observe at least five. First, discipline aims *to expose*. Sin, like cancer, loves to hide. Discipline exposes the cancer so that it might be cut out quickly (see 1 Cor. 5:2).

Second, discipline aims *to warn*. A church does not enact God's retribution through discipline. Rather, it stages a small play that pictures the great judgment to come (v. 5). Discipline is a compassionate warning.

Third, it aims *to save*. Churches pursue discipline when they see a member taking the path toward death, and none of their pleading and arm-waving causes the person to turn around. It's the device of last resort for bringing an individual to repentance (v. 5).

Fourth, discipline aims *to protect*. Just as cancer spreads from one cell to another, so sin quickly spreads from one person to another (v. 6).

Fifth, it aims *to present a good witness for Jesus*. Church discipline, strange to say, is actually good for non-Christians, because it helps to preserve the attractive distinctiveness of God's people (see v. 1). Churches, remember, should be salt and light. "But if the salt loses its saltiness . . . ," Jesus said, "It is no longer good for anything except to be thrown out and trampled by men" (Matt. 5:13, NIV).

THE NEED FOR A GOSPEL FRAMEWORK

It's this last purpose that points to the need for a larger theological framework for knowing how to approach church discipline.

Consider the dilemma raised by the topic of church discipline. Church discipline, we said, centers on the idea of *correcting sin*. But the Christian gospel, most would agree, centers on the idea of *forgiving sin*. If God forgives sin, why would we need to worry about correcting sin? Christians, too, are called to forgive others. What then would be the purpose of correcting one another's sin?

A thinned-out gospel that speaks only of forgiveness and unconditional love does not have the resources for addressing this surface-level tension. As a result, sin goes unaddressed, and churches begin to shadow the world.

However, a more robust gospel addresses not only the guilt-problem of sin, it addresses the corruption-problem of sin with the promise of a new nature. It also places the gospel within the larger biblical story line of God's purposes for humankind to represent him.

God tasked Adam with imaging him through ruling over creation, but Adam failed. So did Israel. So did Israel's king, David. But then came one who imaged God—perfectly. The good news of the gospel is that God has made a way for us to be restored to God and to his original purpose for our lives— reigning together with Jesus over all creation. He promises a pardon from guilt through the work of his Son as well as a new law-obeying nature through the work of his Spirit. It's within this framework that church discipline makes sense, as we now consider.

2

A GOSPEL FRAMEWORK FOR UNDERSTANDING DISCIPLINE

Suppose an American football player joined some friends for a game of soccer. Then, midgame, he reached down and picked up the soccer ball and began to run with it. The referee no doubt would blow his whistle and call a foul.

At this point, the American football player might look back at the referee with bewilderment on his face. Why the whistle? Why the foul? He was simply doing what he always does—grab the ball and run.

In response, one could explain to the American football player that, except for the goalie, soccer players cannot touch the ball with their hands. Now, get back to the game and don't make that mistake again.

Or one could take a little more time to explain how the game of soccer works. Soccer is by definition a game for the feet, not the hands. The very thing which makes soccer fascinating to watch is the ability of skillful players to exert control over the ball without ever using their hands. It's not without reason that every nation in the world except America calls the game "football." The American football player didn't just break a rule; he broke a rule that defines the game's very purpose.

Church discipline, likewise, can be described in two ways. One can describe it as the act of correcting sin, like blowing a whistle against a foul in the Christian life. Or, better, one can try to understand the act of blowing the whistle within the larger framework of the gospel, the church, and the purposes of the Christian life. Placing the act of discipline into this larger theological framework—what I'm calling a gospel framework—will help us exercise the discernment that is inevitably required amidst the many circumstances of sin in a church.

Lying, for instance, is a "foul." Does that mean the whole church needs to get involved every time a member lies? Of course not. So much depends on all the circumstances surrounding the lie or lies: How consequential is it? Is the individual persisting in it? Is it a pattern?

Somewhere there's a line in between a lie worth addressing in private and a lie worth addressing in public. How do we know when that line is crossed? That's the practical challenge of church discipline. That's precisely where so much wisdom is required.

My contention is that church leaders will be better equipped to figure out where that line falls if they understand their corrective activity within a larger gospel framework. The gospel helps us to gauge when to speak and when to stay silent, when to act and when not to act.

WHAT IS THE GOSPEL?

Establishing a framework for church discipline requires us to understand (1) the gospel, (2) what a Christian is, (3) what a local church is, and (4) what church membership means.

What is the gospel? I offered one sketch in the preface. Let me fill it out just a bit here. The gospel is good news that comes at the end of a long story about human beings rebelling against God and enthroning themselves over his world. God created humankind in his image in order to represent his rule and character over creation. He constituted them in his image, so that they could image him. He called them to rule obediently, so that they could rule like he rules: with goodness, justice, holiness, and love.

But humanity decided it was wiser than God, and people chose to rule themselves. They corrupted their own natures and earned the penalty of death. The story of Israel is this creation and fall story writ large. A group of people were given all the advantages of God's law and God's presence for the purposes of representing him, but they did their own thing instead. So he cast them out of his land.

The good news, which comes at the end of this sad story, is that one of Adam's and Israel's sons came to do what neither Adam nor Israel could do: rule obediently and win a people for God. He who was the very image of God came as a man and established a kingdom by obeying the heavenly Father to the utmost. But not only did he establish a kingdom; he won a people for this kingdom by laying down his life as a payment for the guilt of sin, and then rising from the dead and inaugurating a whole new creation.

The good news, in short, is that Jesus Christ has won salvation and rule for all who put their trust in him and follow him as Lord. Salvation includes the forgiveness of sins, reconciliation with God in Christ, reconciliation with Christ's people, and a new Spirit-indwelt heart that now wants to rule obediently for the purposes of representing Jesus on earth.

WHAT IS A CHRISTIAN?

What is a Christian? There are several ways to describe what a Christian is. For starters, it's someone who has been forgiven and united to God through the new covenant in Christ's blood. And it's someone who has been given a new nature by the Spirit (see Deut. 30:6–8; Jeremiah 31; Ezek. 36:24–27).

But there's more to a Christian than a new status and a new nature. A Christian has a new family. He or she, by definition, is now a member of a people. To be reconciled to Christ, by definition, means to be reconciled to Christ's people (Eph. 3:6). Paul makes this connection by linking the first half of Ephesians 2 with the second half. First, he tells us that we have been saved by grace (Eph. 1:1–10). Second, he tells us that the dividing wall of partition between Jew and Gentile has fallen, creating one new man (vv. 11–22). To be adopted by a mother and father is to be given a whole new set of brothers and sisters. So it is with Christianity. Whether we were aware that we were joining a new family or not, our adoption into Christ is an adoption into a family.

So a Christian has a new status, a new nature, a new family, and, finally, a new job description. A Christian is someone who now represents Jesus and therefore God. This is precisely the message of baptism and the Lord's Supper. To be baptized is to identify ourselves with the name of the Father, the Son, and the Holy Spirit, as well as to identify ourselves with Christ's death and resurrection (Matt. 28:19; Rom. 6:4–5). To receive the Lord's Supper is to proclaim his death and our membership in his body (1 Cor. 11:26–29; see Matt. 26:26–29). God wants his people to be known and marked off. He wants a line between his people and the world. He wants us to be holy because he is holy. Christians represent him now—today!

A Christian, in other words, is someone who wears the name of God on earth, who declares his gospel, and who is united to his people. In essence, the Christian is an ambassador—someone whose identity and work meld together. Everything that an ambassador is, says, and does represents his or her king. So it is with Christians and Christ.

WHAT IS A LOCAL CHURCH?

How about the local church? What is it? A local church is more than just a gathering of Christians. Ten Christians sitting together in the park do not constitute a church. Jesus has given a kingdom authority to Christians gathered together as a local church that he has not given to individual Christians. Specifically, he has given local churches the authority to exercise the keys of the kingdom through giving and withholding baptism and the Lord's Supper, thereby doing the work of marking off God's people from the world.

This is the picture we first get in Matthew 16 and 18, and then in Matthew 28; this picture then turns into a motion picture in the book of Acts and the Epistles. Jesus authorizes the local church to use the keys of the kingdom to stand in front of a confessor, to consider the confessor's confession, to consider his or her life, and to announce an official judgment on heaven's behalf. Is that the right confession? Is this a true confessor? The local church follows Jesus's example of questioning Peter, who declared that Jesus was the Christ (Matt. 16:16–17). Specifically, the church carries out its task through the ordinances that are established in Matthew 26 and Matthew 28: the Lord's Supper and baptism.[1]

The local church, in other words, has heaven's authority for declaring who is a kingdom citizen and therefore represents Jesus's name on earth. Jesus has not authorized individual people to suddenly decide that they're Christians, and to then stand before the nations and declare that they represent Jesus. The people of Jerusalem ask Peter what they had to do to be saved. He replied, "Repent and be baptized" (Acts 2:38). They needed the Jerusalem church's official affirmation.

We should remember that the local church's power is declaratory. A church does not *make* someone a citizen of the kingdom. But it does have the responsibility for declaring who does and who does not belong to Christ's kingdom. A church, then, is like the embassy of a nation. If your passport expires while traveling in a foreign country, you apply to the

---

[1] I offer a longer explanation and defense for my interpretation of these passages and the definitions offered here in chapter 3 of *Church Membership: How the World Knows Who Represents Jesus* (Wheaton, IL: Crossway, 2012). An even fuller defense can be found in chapter 4 of my *The Church and the Surprising Offense of God's Love: Reintroducing the Doctrines of Membership and Discipline* (Wheaton, IL: Crossway, 2010).

embassy of your country to have your passport renewed. The embassy has an authority that you as an individual citizen do not have.

Of course, the church is more than an institution with kingdom authority. It's also a "body," a "family," a "flock," a "temple," a "pillar and buttress of truth," and more. But we must not overlook the fact that it is also the *institution* on earth *instituted* by Jesus with authority for declaring who his citizens or ambassadors are.

To define the local church institutionally, then, we could say that it is a group of Christians who regularly gather in Christ's name to officially affirm and oversee one another's membership in Jesus Christ and his kingdom through gospel preaching and gospel ordinances.

As such, Christians do not "join" churches like they join clubs, they submit to them. The church is not an absolute authority, any more than a parent is an absolute authority for a child. But Christ does want Christians to submit to the oversight of local churches by virtue of their citizenship in his kingdom.

Will the local church exercise the keys perfectly? No. It will make mistakes, just like every other authority established by Jesus makes mistakes. The local church is an imperfect representation of Christ's end-time gathering. But the fact that it makes mistakes, just like presidents and parents do, does not mean it is without an authoritative mandate.

In all of this, is should be clear that one of the church's primary jobs is to protect the name of Jesus.

WHAT IS CHURCH MEMBERSHIP?

What then is church membership? It's a declaration of citizenship in Christ's kingdom. It's a passport. It's an announcement made in the pressroom of Christ's kingdom. It's the declaration that a professing individual is an official, licensed, card-carrying, bona fide Jesus representative.

More concretely, church membership is a formal relationship between a local church and a Christian characterized by the church's affirmation and oversight of a Christian's discipleship and the Christian's submission to living out his or her discipleship in the care of the church.

Notice that several elements are present:

- a church body formally *affirms* an individual's profession of faith and baptism as credible;
- it promises *to give oversight* to that individual's discipleship;
- the individual formally *submits* his or her discipleship to the service and authority of this body and its leaders.

The church body says to the individual, "We recognize your profession of faith, baptism, and discipleship to Christ as valid. Therefore, we publicly *affirm* and acknowledge you before the nations as belonging to Christ, and we extend the *oversight* of our fellowship." Principally, the individual says to the church body, "Insofar as I recognize you as a faithful, gospel-declaring church, I *submit* my presence and my discipleship to your love and oversight."

The standards for church membership should be no higher or lower than the standards for being a Christian, with one exception. A Christian is someone who has repented and believed, and that's who churches should affirm as members. The only additional requirement is baptism. Church members must be baptized, a pattern that is uniform in the New Testament. Peter said to the crowds in Jerusalem, "Repent and be baptized" (Acts 2:38). And Paul, writing to the church in Rome, simply assumes that everyone who belongs to the Roman church has been baptized (Rom. 6:1–3).

Church membership, in other words, is not about "additional requirements." It's about a church taking specific responsibility for a Christian, and a Christian for a church. It's about "putting on," "embodying," "living out," and "making concrete" our membership in Christ's universal body. In some ways, the union which constitutes a local church and its members is like the "I do" of a marriage ceremony, which is why some refer to church membership as a "covenant."

It's true that a Christian must choose to join a church, but that does not make it a voluntary organization. Having chosen Christ, a Christian has no choice but to choose to join a church.

A FULLER CONCEPT OF CHURCH DISCIPLINE

The preceding discussion on the gospel, the Christian, the church, and church membership provides the framework through which church discipline should be understood. Let me draw out four elements from this discussion that provide important foundational assumptions for church discipline:

1) *An expectation of transformation.* The new covenant promises that Christ's people will live transformed lives through the

power of the Spirit. Even if change comes slowly, churches should expect change—the visible fruit of God's grace and Spirit. Discipline is the right response to a lack of visible fruit, or, even more, the presence of bad fruit.

2) *The work of representation.* Christians are to be little Christs, representing Jesus on earth. The concept of representation depends on the idea that Jesus is Savior *and* Lord; it depends on the fact that Christians are given a new status *and* a new work. Discipline is the right response when Christians fail to represent Jesus and show no desire for doing so.

3) *The local church's authority.* Jesus gave the local church the authority of the keys to officially affirm and oversee citizens of his kingdom. Churches do not *make* people Christians. The Spirit does that. But churches have the declarative authority and responsibility for making public statements before the nations about who is and isn't a Christian. A church's act of excommunication, therefore, does not consist of physically and forcibly removing the individual from its public gatherings, as if the church had the state's power of the sword to physically move people's bodies; rather, it consists of the public statement that it can no longer vouch for an individual's citizenship in heaven. Excommunication is a church's declaration that it can no longer affirm that an individual is a Christian.

4) *Membership as submission.* Christians are called, as a matter of obedience to Christ, to submit to the affirmation and oversight of local churches. When threatened by a possible act of discipline, therefore, church members cannot simply preempt the church's action with a resignation. That would be analogous to an individual resigning his national citizenship before a court could prosecute the criminal activity for which he had been indicted.

When we view church discipline through this theological

grid, we gain a fuller understanding. It's not just about correcting sin or blowing whistles. It's about correcting sin for the purposes of ensuring that church members are indeed representing Jesus rightly. It's about calling them to be what they claim to be.

Discipline therefore revolves around the question of who on earth is licensed or authorized to represent heaven. To call oneself a Christian is to profess to have that right. To be a church member is to be formally affirmed as having that right. The local church, Jesus's key-carrying institution, vouches for the credibility of a Christian's profession through baptism and the Lord's Supper. Church discipline comes into play whenever that credibility is called into question. It's driven by a single question: does the church still believe an erring member is really a Christian, such that it's willing to continue declaring so publicly?

In short, church discipline is all about the reputation of Jesus on earth. The stakes are high indeed.

3

WHEN IS DISCIPLINE NECESSARY?

A Christian disciple is someone who follows Jesus Christ. Discipleship in the local church involves church members helping one another follow Jesus. Members do this through formation and correction. They teach the good and correct the bad. They encourage one another toward the right path, and help keep one another off the wrong path.

Along these lines, a Christian's need for correction should make sense to us. A basic part of being a Christian is admitting that we are finite and fallen. We can be both unaware and self-deceived. Therefore we need other believers to help us know when we have stepped off the path of discipleship.

I remember having a conversation about my income taxes with another elder in my church, Jamie. Somewhere in the conversation, Jamie mentioned something about paying taxes on the rental income that my wife and I were receiving from the person living in our basement. The very second that Jamie said the words "rental income" the thought popped into my head, "Wait a second, rental *income*? I need to pay taxes on those rent checks, don't I?" Effectively, I had been stealing from the United States government, and I didn't know it. I had departed from the path of discipleship and was failing to represent Jesus, who said we should pay our taxes to Caesar. Therefore, as a Christian, I had no choice but to go back and open up the previous year's taxes and pay the additional money.

As Christians who admit we are finite and fallen, we can also admit that there may be many areas in which our lives are out of step with Jesus. The solution, then, is to begin opening up our lives to other members of the church. They can then help us see what we cannot immediately see about ourselves.

And that's what discipline is all about: helping one another grow in Christlikeness by correcting sin. I don't know if Jamie meant to "discipline" me, but thankfully, that's what he was doing.

When shall we say that church discipline is necessary? Broadly speaking, discipline is necessary whenever a disciple departs from the way of Christ by sinning. It's necessary whenever a gap opens up between a Christian's profession and life, and the so-called representative of Jesus fails to represent Jesus.

Most often, discipline occurs informally and privately. A brother or sister in Christ sins, and another brother or sister, with love, quietly addresses the matter.

Occasionally, the process occurs formally and publicly, which is what people most often mean when they refer to "church discipline," and certainly what we mean by excommunication. Formal church discipline is the appropriate course of action whenever a church member's failure to represent

Jesus becomes so characteristic and habitual that the church no longer believes he or she is a Christian. The church must then remove its affirmation of a person's profession of faith. This is the "gospel framework" approach to discipline that we considered in the last chapter. It's not driven by lists of which sins qualify for discipline. It's driven by the single question of whether a church can continue to publicly affirm a person's profession of faith as credible.

Within this framework, can we say anything more specific about when church discipline is necessary?

SINS WE EXPECT, SINS WE DON'T

A moment ago I intimated that there's a line in between sins that might be addressed privately and sins that require the whole congregation to become involved. Here is a parallel observation: somewhere there is a line in between sins that you expect of Christians, and sins which make you think that someone may not be a Christian. Informal and private discipline occurs on both sides of the line, to be sure. But formal church discipline or excommunication is warranted, broadly speaking, when an individual crosses from the first domain to the second, from sins we expect to sins we don't.

There's a difference, for instance, between an ordinary lie that is repented of, and a lie that a person builds a life upon and refuses to relinquish. For instance, compare the lies of two different professing Christians. The first boasts about receiving a prestigious job offer that he never received; later, he confesses the lie. The second builds an entire career on falsified information; later, he's confronted, but he persists in

49

the fabrications. The first lie is the kind of sin that—as much as we wish it were not the case—we occasionally expect from Christians. The "old man," to use Paul's language, pops up in a believer's head and tries to dominate the "new man," but the new man fights back. The second lie is *not* something we expect from a person in whom the Holy Spirit dwells. There's no evidence of a struggle between an old man and a new. There's just the old.

Christians who are indwelt by the Holy Spirit, generally speaking, cannot abide for long in known sin. They eventually become so uncomfortable—courtesy of the Spirit—that they eventually do the right thing.

Formal church discipline or excommunication is warranted when an individual seems to happily abide in known sin. There's no evidence that the Spirit is making him or her uncomfortable, other than the discomfort of getting caught. Rather, obedience to sin's desires are *characteristic*.

All sin is wrong. All sin misrepresents Jesus. But some sins or sin patterns will cause a whole assembly of people to lose trust in a person's profession of faith. At some point, a person's words lose credibility. The member might claim to be "repentant" or "just fine" or "not disobeying *that* bad," but for whatever reason the church can no longer believe these words. The life behind them is too contradictory. So the church removes its public affirmation by barring the member from the Lord's Table. It takes away his passport and announces that it can no longer formally affirm the individual's citizenship in Christ's kingdom.

PASTORAL AND SITUATIONAL SENSITIVITY

Viewing church discipline through this gospel framework—
a framework driven not by lists of sins but by the question
of whether the church can continue to affirm a profession
of faith—allows for greater pastoral sensitivity in moving
from situation to situation. Scripture is always our guide for
what counts as a sin, but pastoral care is needed to determine
which sins require discipline, and to what extent.

Two different people might commit the same sin, but a
host of circumstances will affect a pastor and a church's sense
of what that sin means. An accountant who evades paying
taxes presents a larger problem than others who might in
ignorance do the same, because an accountant knows exactly
what he's doing and means to do it. An unmarried couple
caught in fornication for the fifth time is probably more
deserving of discipline than an unmarried couple caught for
the first time. And brand-new Christians, in general, can be
expected to stumble into major sin more often than seasoned
believers.

As subjective as it sounds, different situational factors
will affect what we *expect* of a Christian. And expectation has
a role to play because we live in the overlap of the present
age and the coming age. In this age, Christians are, as Martin
Luther said, simultaneously sinful and justified. We *expect*
the new man and old man to do battle against one another,
and we recognize that different circumstances (e.g., age in
the faith; amount of teaching one has received) may well give
either the new man or the old man the upper hand in any given
situation. As such, church discipline is never just about the

question, "Which sin?" as if we had a weight scale that could tell us if a sin is heavy enough to warrant discipline. Rather, sins get weighed in a balance, with the sin on the one side of the balance and the evidences of repentance on the other side—and not just repentance from the particular sin, but an overall posture of repentance in the person's life. Evaluating a prospective discipline case, therefore, is always about evaluating the dynamic between a person's overall profession of repentance and the sins that weigh against that profession, calling it into question.

Instructive along these lines is Jesus's requirement in Matthew 18 to establish a matter with two or three witnesses before taking it to the church (Matt. 18:16). The passage from which he quotes, Deuteronomy 19, shows that God meant for the Israelites to take great care in ensuring that a criminal prosecution proceeded carefully and fairly. Jesus likewise meant for church leaders and members to judge each matter carefully. They should consider the evidence, the different sides of the story, and the extenuating circumstances. There should be no rush to judgment. Christians should move slowly, thoughtfully, and graciously.

The gauge by which the two or three witnesses (and eventually the church) should measure the sin or sin pattern is a simple one: does the person repeatedly refuse to repent, such that the person's profession eventually becomes unbelievable and not affirmable? That is, does this person clench his or her fist around this sin so tightly that it outweighs all other protestations of faith?

At the same time, a whole host of other situational elements should factor into a church's deliberations:

- How long has he been a Christian?
- What teaching has he received?
- Does the sinner admit his action was wrong?
- Does he seem genuinely grieved over his sin, or is there a tone of annoyance in his confession?
- Did he quickly confess, or did we have to drag out the information?
- Was he immediately forthcoming with all of his sins, or did we have to dig them out one by one?
- Is it likely that he's still hiding information?
- Is this a pattern? Is this characteristic?
- Is he inviting correction?
- Is he welcoming counsel for how to fight against the sin, or does he reject counsel, convinced that he knows best how to deal with it?
- As we discuss his sin, does it feel like he's standing on our side against the sin, or is he defensive? In other words, is he saying, "Yeah, you're absolutely right. It's awful. What should I do?" Or is he saying, "Yeah, fine. Okay. We'll see."
- Are there factors in his personal or family history that make the sin not less wrong but more likely?
- Was he led into sin by others whom he reasonably trusted?

The answer to any one of these questions may not push a church or church leader's judgment in one direction or another. But it might, and the host of these factors together often do affect whether we continue to view someone as a Christian even as they sin.

OUTWARD, SERIOUS, UNREPENTANT

Jesus's use of Deuteronomy 19 and Paul's telling the Corinthians to "judge" and to "try cases" (1 Cor. 5:12; 6:2–5) instructs us in at least two more ways. First, Jesus *does* mean for churches to exercise judgment in the manner we have been describing, even though he forbids a self-righteous, personal-vendetta kind of judgment among Christians elsewhere (Matt. 7:1–2).

Second, the processes of judgment in a church, as in a courtroom, depend on what people can see with their eyes or hear with their ears. God has not given Christians X-ray eyes for seeing into hearts. He's given Christians—as he's given all human beings—eyes, ears, and brains that can be used to consider the fruit of individual lives and to exercise discernment (1 Cor. 5:12; see Matt. 3:8; 7:16–20; 12:33; 21:43). Non-Christians are surely using their eyes, ears, and brains to observe Christian lives and assess them; Christians should do the same. That's part of protecting the name of Jesus, not to mention part of loving the sinner, the non-Christian onlookers, and the church.

Jesus gives churches the authority to make *public* declarations based precisely on the *public* or outward fruit of people's lives.

In other words, I believe we can say a little bit more about which sins should be disciplined by a church beyond "when the sin crosses the line from expected to unexpected." It does help to establish some kind of minimum standard even if it's not theoretically foolproof. Formal church discipline should occur with sins that are *outward*, *serious*, and *unrepentant*.

First, a sin must have an *outward* manifestation. Churches should not throw the red flag of ejection every time they suspect greed or pride in someone's heart. It must be something that can be seen with the eyes or heard with the ears.

Second, a sin must be *serious*. A church and its leaders should not pursue every sin to the utmost. There needs to be some place in a church's life for love to "cover a multitude of sins" (1 Pet. 4:8). Thankfully, God does not perceptibly discipline us every time we sin.

Finally, a sin must be *unrepented of*. The person involved has been confronted with God's commands in Scripture, but he or she refuses to let go of the sin. From all appearances, the person prizes the sin more than Jesus.

More or less, all three of these factors should be present before a church moves toward excommunication.

WHY DIFFERENT APPROACHES FROM JESUS AND PAUL?

There is one more knotty issue we need to consider concerning *when* to discipline. And it's a pebble that will start an avalanche of confusion if we're not careful. That's the question of why Paul's approach in 1 Corinthians 5 appears to be so different from Jesus's approach in Matthew 18.

In 1 Corinthians 5, we recall, Paul rebukes a church for tolerating a sin "of a kind that is not tolerated even among pagans, for a man has his father's wife" (1 Cor. 5:1). He does not tell the church to warn the man in order to see if he might be brought to repentance. He just tells them to "remove" the man (v. 2). There's no testing the waters of repentance. There's no conversation between the man and the elders. There's just

55

a call to immediate action: "Purge the evil person from among you" (v. 13). Jesus on the other hand advised churches to offer several warnings along the road to excommunication, each of which presents an off-ramp for the process.

The temptation is to explain the different approaches by saying that Jesus and Paul have different kinds of sin in mind, which means that we in turn should adopt one process or another according to the kind of sin involved. Jesus uses the example of an ordinary interpersonal sin, while Paul uses a heavy-duty sin. We should likewise adopt the former process for the smaller stuff and the latter process for the heavier stuff.

Writers on church discipline in the eighteenth and nineteenth centuries sometimes went in this direction. They observed two things about the 1 Corinthians 5 episode: first, the sin was publicly scandalous ("not tolerated even among pagans"); second, Paul's call for immediate excommunication—no warnings given—suggests that he was not concerned in the short term with whether the man was repentant, again, because of the sin's scandalous nature. Jesus's reputation was of greater value, and so the church had to act in order to preserve Christ's reputation, even if the individual was repentant.

I am surely sympathetic with the concern for the reputation of Christ, as my entire framework for approaching discipline should make clear. But I don't find this historic explanation compelling for a couple of reasons. For starters, it makes the decision of whether to excommunicate dependent on the standards of the world, which are not holy and are always changing. One society's scandal is another society's badge of honor (think of abortion or homosexuality). Also, excommunicating people whom a church believes to be repentant would mean handing Christians over to Satan's kingdom. Wouldn't that be unjust to the Christian and dishonest to the world? Churches should not excommunicate people whom they believe are Christians. Doing so is essentially legalistic, because it makes the criteria for church membership not "repentance and faith" but "repentance, faith, and never-committing-sin-*x*."

Paul's approach in 1 Corinthians surely does open up an exit doorway for us that is not exactly visible in Matthew 18—the doorway of immediate excommunication. And this is indeed a doorway we will use most often for the "really big" sins. But we must remember not to focus exclusively on the "heaviness" of a sin. Remember, the decision to move toward excommunication is always about examining the dynamic between the sin and a person's overall posture of repentance. It's not a sin scale that we need; it's a sin-versus-repentance balance. After all, repentant Christians do sin. The question is always, why would *this* sin counterbalance our assumption of specific and general repentance? And answering that question always requires us to look at both sides of the balance with pastoral and situational sensitivity.

So what are the criteria of immediate excommunication? A more careful examination of 1 Corinthians 5 and 6 will help us find the answer. Consider the following texts:

> **5:1–2** It is actually reported that there is sexual immorality among you, and of a kind that is not tolerated even among

pagans, for a man has his father's wife. And you are arrogant! Ought you not rather to mourn?

5:4–5 When you are assembled in the name of the Lord Jesus . . . you are to deliver this man to Satan for the destruction of the flesh.

5:9–11 I wrote to you in my letter not to associate with sexually immoral people—not at all meaning the sexually immoral of this world, or the greedy and swindlers, or idolaters, since then you would need to go out of the world. But now I am writing to you not to associate with anyone who bears the name of brother if he is guilty of sexual immorality or greed, or is an idolater, reviler, drunkard, or swindler—not even to eat with such a one.

5:12 Is it not those inside the church whom you are to judge?

5:13 Purge the evil person from among you.

6:9–11 Do you not know that the unrighteous will not inherit the kingdom of God? Do not be deceived: neither the sexually immoral, nor idolaters, nor adulterers, nor men who practice homosexuality, nor thieves, nor the greedy, nor drunkards, nor revilers, nor swindlers will inherit the kingdom of God. And such were some of you. But you were washed, you were sanctified, you were justified in the name of the Lord Jesus Christ and by the Spirit of our God.

The man's sin in 5:1 may indeed be "publicly scandalous" or "really bad," but that's not the point. Rather, Paul is laying out two categories of people in these texts: those who are characteristically repentant and those who are not. The characteristically repentant belong inside the church; the characteristically unrepentant do not because they will not inherit the kingdom of God.

It might be easier to see this if we move backward through the texts above. The last one shows the two categories clearly: there are the "unrighteous" who will not inherit the kingdom of God, and there is the church, which is comprised of individuals who have been changed: "And such were some of you." On the unrighteous side, Paul does not simply describe particular sins, he describes people who are *defined by* those sins. He doesn't use adjectives, he uses nouns: "the sexual immoral," "the greedy," "the idolaters," "the slanderers," "the drunkards," and "the swindlers" (1 Cor. 6:9–11). These sins *characterize* these people. It's what they *are*. The same characterization is evident in the last sentence of chapter 5: "Purge the evil person from among you" (5:13). The man is "evil." A person like that, says the verse that comes just before it, does not belong in the church (5:12).

It's not difficult to see that Paul means to link the lists in chapter 5 and 6 insofar as he lists the same kinds of sinners: the sexually immoral, the greedy, the idolaters, the revilers, the drunkards, or the swindlers (5:9–11). (We should not assume this is an exhaustive list. Chapter 6 even adds a couple more categories. It is instead a typical list.) Again, the church must not share fellowship with people who are characteristically unrepentant: "I wrote to you in my letter not to associate with sexually immoral people" (v. 9).

And that's exactly what this man in chapter 5 is: characteristically unrepentant. He must be handed over to Satan for the destruction of his flesh because his flesh still has the upper hand in his life (5:5). The church has not been condemning his actions but approving it (5:2). Yet he is certainly sexually immoral (5:1).

In short, Paul means for this man to be excluded because he is *characteristically unrepentant*. Present signs indicate that he will not inherit the kingdom of God, and therefore the church must cast him out now so that his soul might be warned and saved. Did Paul have more information on this guy than we do? Perhaps. It's not entirely clear to us *how* Paul arrived at this conclusion about the individual, but that's the conclusion he arrived at nonetheless: he's not a Christian. He is "evil" (5:13). He belongs to the category of the "unrighteous" (6:9).

At this point, the differences between Jesus's approach in Matthew 18 and Paul's approach in 1 Corinthians 5 should be more evident. Paul's assumptions about the man *begin* just short of where Jesus's process *ends*. Paul begins with the assumption of an unyielding unrepentance. Jesus's process exists for the purpose of determining whether or not a person is unyieldingly unrepentant—for determining what Paul takes as a given.

Another difference in the two passages lies in how widely the information is known and agreed upon. In Matthew 18, one person thinks there is a sin, but then he needs two or three others to agree with him. After that, he needs the whole church to agree. In 1 Corinthians 5, on the other hand, the whole church knows what's happening. Again, it begins just short of where Matthew 18 ends.

So churches should not simply address average sins using the Matthew 18 model and really big sins using the 1 Corinthians 5 model. Rather, churches must always look at both sides of the "sin vs. repentance" balance scale. Even when a person's sin seems big, the church still needs to be convinced that the person is characteristically unrepentant. And a church may not be convinced at the moment in which the sin is exposed. Members still might feel the need to have some conversations, and to offer a challenge or warning.

It's not difficult to imagine situations in which a church member is guilty of one of the sins listed in 1 Corinthians 5 or 6, but in which the church rightly determines to use a Matthew 18 process. Imagine, for example, that someone in your church has committed an act or even multiple acts of drunkenness or various forms of sexual immorality. I believe that in some cases there's an opportunity for a series of warnings, as in Matthew 18, before excommunication occurs.

What then do we make of Paul's observation: this man's sin "is not tolerated even among pagans"? There's no denying that the man's sin is publicly scandalous, but to me Paul's words sound like an exclamatory smack to the head intended to wake up the Corinthians. They don't see something that they plainly should see. Paul's words don't sound like a theologian trying to craft a whole separate category of sin that changes all the rules on church membership and excommunication. If he were, I suspect he'd offer more than one clipped phrase.

A DISQUALIFIED PROFESSION

Here's one more way to view the entire episode in 1 Corinthians 5. There are, no doubt, some sins that are so deliberate (like a long pattern of abuse or murder) or repugnant (like sexually predatory behavior or extortion) that any quick words of apology would be unbelievable. It's not that such sins cannot be forgiven, or that a person might not be immediately repentant. But some time needs to pass and the fruit of repentance displayed before a church can responsibly pronounce forgiveness (see the example in Acts 8:17–24). A church cannot responsibly believe the words of a member who has been willfully living in a habitual sin. It's almost as if the nature of some sins "disables" a church's ability to continue affirming the person's overall posture of repentance, and so the church has no choice but to remove its affirmation for the time being. The sin pushes its side of the balance straight down and the evidence of repentance side straight up. All the positive evidence is immediately undermined because the sin involves so much deceit.

There are some sins that we really would *not expect* a Christian to do. And to do them means one is probably not a Christian, or at least that's how the church will treat the individual until the church's trust can once again be earned. It could be that Paul viewed a man who would sleep with his father's wife in this way.

Years ago I met regularly with a young man who, last year, I learned had been arrested for a shameful form of criminal activity. It even made the local news. He had been secretly engaged in the activity for more than a year while actively serving at his church. When the church learned about the sin through the man's arrest, it acted swiftly to remove him from membership. The man wept and claimed to be sorry, but because he had been living a grotesque double life, the church could not trust his words of repentance, at least for a time. It chose to test his repentance not *before* the act of excommunication, but *after*. I believe the church was correct to do so. The man's action was a threat both to other sheep and to the witness of Christ in the world, making the whole situation more urgent. The church was right to discipline him swiftly, because "the unrighteous will not inherit the kingdom of God" (1 Cor. 6:9).

Ultimately, I believe the combination of Matthew 18 and 1 Corinthians 5 suggests that churches need to arrive at one of three conclusions before determining that it's time to act:

- When a church becomes convinced that a person is genuinely repentant, it should not proceed with any form of discipline (and I cannot think of a single exception to this principle).
- When a church becomes convinced that a person is characteristically (not temporarily) unrepentant, it should proceed with excommunication.
- When a sin is so deliberate, repugnant, and indicative of a deep double-mindedness that a congregation is left unable to give credence to a profession of repentance, at least until time has passed and trust has been re-earned, it should proceed with excommunication, determining to test for repentance after the fact.

PURITY OR POVERTY OF SPIRIT

If church discipline is the appropriate course of action when-ever a representative of Jesus fails to represent Jesus, should churches expect moral perfection?

In some respects, this is exactly the standard that Jesus enunciates. In Matthew 5 he tells us that a Christian's righ-teousness must exceed that of the scribes and Pharisees, lest he or she never enter the kingdom of heaven (Matt. 5:20). Later in the chapter, he tells us that a Christian must be perfect like the heavenly Father is perfect (v. 48). Churches should strive to represent Jesus's perfection indeed!

But Jesus was also deeply realistic and understanding, which is why Matthew 5 begins with the beloved Beatitudes:

> Blessed are the poor in spirit, for theirs is the kingdom of heaven.
> Blessed are those who mourn, for they shall be comforted.
> Blessed are the meek, for they shall inherit the earth.
> Blessed are those who hunger and thirst for righteousness, for they shall be satisfied.
> Blessed are the merciful, for they shall receive mercy.
> Blessed are the pure in heart, for they shall see God.
> Blessed are the peacemakers, for they shall be called sons of God.
> Blessed are those who are persecuted for righteousness' sake, for theirs is the kingdom of heaven. (Matt. 5:3–10)

Who on earth represents the kingdom of heaven? Who gets to see God and be called a son of God? In one sense, it's those who look and act like their heavenly Father, like sons generally do. Both the divine Father and the divine Son are merciful, pure in heart, and peacemaking. And the divine Son was certainly persecuted for righteousness' sake. Churches, too, should look to affirm the sons who are all of these things.

But in a fallen world, the sons of God are also those who recognize their spiritual poverty, who mourn their sin, who meekly let go of their demands, and who hunger and thirst for the righteousness, which they know they lack. Churches, therefore, should not be surprised whenever their Jesus-representing members sin; but they should be deeply interested in how their members respond to that sin. Do they mourn? Do they hunger and thirst for righteousness?

In other words, true representatives of Jesus will be two things: increasingly pure *and* increasingly poor in spirit amidst remaining impurity (see also 2 Cor. 7:11). Churches, in their work of exercising the keys of the kingdom, must look for both.

I once asked a former pastor of mine for counsel on how to respond to a friend who had taken tentative steps toward an adulterous affair, which, gratefully, was intercepted before it came to full fruition. My pastor advised me, "It's not surprising that this man would be tempted toward this sin. The real question is, how will he respond to your rebuke? It's his response to correction that will reveal where his heart truly lies."

4

HOW DOES A CHURCH PRACTICE DISCIPLINE?

Formal public discipline works best in a church culture where informal and private discipline is welcomed and practiced. If you try swinging the broad, blunt sword of excommunication before members recognize their general need to hold one another accountable, you are asking for a fight.

Accountability within a church is an implication of the gospel, and that accountability should ultimately be practiced throughout a church's life, both publicly and privately. But when people are not accustomed to being held accountable for their sin, it's surely easier to begin with private accountability than with public.

Public accountability should be an outgrowth of what's already going on in the private lives of church members.

I have one pastor friend who was trying to persuade his fellow elders to bring a case of discipline before the church. A man had left his wife. But the elders weren't sure if the congregation was ready to exclude someone, and so they moved slowly—perhaps too slowly. When the elders did finally recommend excommunication, the congregation essentially responded, "It's about time. We knew we were supposed to do something in these cases." In other words, the elders had done a good job of cultivating the right culture for discipline within the church.

Formal church discipline works best when members already know how to give and receive loving correction. They do it in their homes. They do it over lunch. They do it gently, carefully, and always with the good of the other person in mind. They don't offer corrective words selfishly—just to "get something off the chest."

Here are five other principles for how to conduct church discipline, based on what we see in the New Testament.

THE PROCESS SHOULD INVOLVE AS FEW PEOPLE AS POSSIBLE

A clear principle that emerges from Matthew 18:15–20 is that Jesus means for the process of correcting sin to involve as few people as necessary for producing repentance. If a one-on-one encounter yields repentance, good. If it takes two or three more, then leave it at that. A matter should only be taken to the whole church when all other avenues have been exhausted.

The Matthew 18 process, of course, presumes that a broader circle doesn't already know about the sin in question. Sins that are already public in nature, as in 1 Corinthians 5, may require the church leaders to say something to the entire church. A similar situation is in view in Philippians 4, when Paul, in front of the whole church, entreats Euodia and Syntche to agree with one another (Phil. 4:2–3). Presumably, the church already knew of the disagreement.

Sometimes a sin will have public consequences that need to be publicly addressed, even if the individual proves privately repentant. This may be the case, for instance, when a woman becomes pregnant out of wedlock. The church leaders might decide that she and her partner (if he's in the church) are genuinely repentant and therefore not move toward formal discipline. But they still might tenderly address the matter with the church (1) so that they can teach positively about a Christian view of sexuality over and against the couple's example and (2) so that the leaders can testify to God's grace in the couple's repentance, while also calling the church to embrace and serve the couple and their child. Like it or not, saying nothing in such a situation teaches the church that sin is no big deal, and it also leaves the church to guess and gossip about the couple. Saying nothing can even breed mistrust and disunity.

The twin priorities that undergird the principle of keeping the process of discipline as small as possible are a desire for the sinner's repentance and a desire to protect the name of Jesus.

CHURCH LEADERS SHOULD LEAD THE PROCESS

Sin is deceitful and complex. It's not without reason, therefore, that Paul writes, "Brothers, if anyone is caught in any transgression, you who are spiritual should restore him in a spirit of gentleness. Keep watch on yourself, lest you too be tempted" (Gal. 6:1). Paul knows that younger sheep can be easily deceived, tempted either to join the sinner in sin or at least to be persuaded by the sinner's arguments for why the sin is acceptable. Therefore, Paul entreats the "spiritual" to lead in the rescue.

Paul's reference to the "spiritual" does not necessarily mean the church's elders, or he would have said "elders." It does suggest that members do well to involve older and wiser brothers and sisters in the faith when an initial one-on-one encounter goes nowhere. Generally speaking, it probably will be the church elders who are consulted and then called upon to lead the process of discipline, particularly when the process expands to broader and broader circles.

Insofar as God has given elders oversight over the whole church, I would certainly recommend that any sin that is taken before the whole church should first go to the elders.

THE LENGTH OF THE PROCESS DEPENDS ON HOW LONG IT TAKES TO ESTABLISH CHARACTERISTIC UNREPENTANCE

One of the more difficult questions in practicing discipline surely must be, is now the time to proceed to the next level? Sometimes Scripture presents the process of discipline as moving slowly, such as Matthew 18, which calls for at least three warnings before a person is removed. Sometimes it presents it as moving quickly, as in 1 Corinthians 5 where Paul calls for immediate removal. And then there is Titus 3:10, which seems like it lands in between the two. It calls for two warnings before proceeding to removal.

As we saw in chapter 3, the key difference between Matthew 18 and 1 Corinthians 5 is that they represent two different stages in the overall excommunication process. First Corinthians 5 begins where Matthew 18 ends, with the determination of characteristic unrepentance of a sin or sin pattern that is known throughout the church. When a church determines that an individual is characteristically unrepentant, excommunication should follow.

From a theoretical standpoint, therefore, it's fairly simple to describe how long the process of discipline should last: however long it takes the church to conclude that an individual is characteristically unrepentant. Church members might look at the evidence and arrive at the conclusion in a minute. They might spend months sifting through the evidence and engaging in countless conversations in the attempt to arrive at a clear conviction and a common mind. The question of "how long" is not difficult for theoretical reasons; it's difficult for real-life reasons. We cannot see into people's hearts, and we feel the burden of being tremendously careful whenever we are called upon to inspect the fruit and make a determination on a matter as important as whether the church can continue testifying that someone belongs to the kingdom of God.

Ironically, since medium-sized sins don't weigh as heavily against the repentance side of the balance, the process tends to move slower. Take substance addiction as an example. It doesn't immediately discredit a person's profession of faith. But it does raise a question mark and puts a church in the position of needing to do the slow, careful work of testing for repentance. This is another lesson we can learn from the centrifugal movement that Jesus presents in Matthew 18. Every time the number of people involved becomes a little broader, the sinner is once more confronted with the question, "Are you *sure* you still want to hold onto this sin?"

Humans can sometimes fool themselves into believing that they can have both Jesus *and* their favorite sin. It takes several rounds of escalating confrontations to help them realize, "No, I cannot. It's one or the other."

A few verses before Jesus's instruction in Matthew 18 about church discipline, he provides us with help for determining whether an individual is characteristically repentant: would the person be willing to cut off a hand or tear out an eye rather than repeat the sin (Matt. 18:8–9)? That is to say, is he or she willing to do whatever it takes to fight against the sin? Repenting people, typically, are zealous about casting off their sin. That's what God's Spirit does inside of them. When this happens, one can expect to see a willingness to accept outside counsel. A willingness to inconvenience their schedules. A willingness to confess embarrassing things. A willingness to make financial sacrifices or lose friends or end relationships.

On the other hand, the bigger or more blatant a sin or sin pattern is, the more heavily it weighs against the repentance side of the balance.[2] It more quickly discredits a person's profession of faith, and may lead a church to act more quickly. There's a difference, for instance, between discovering that someone is a serial adulterer and that someone is an alcoholic. Both sins will undermine the credibility of one's profession of faith, but I dare say the former sin will do this more quickly than the latter.

Typically, larger sins are accompanied by one form of

---

[2] What's a "bigger" sin? It's a sin that more quickly and visibly destroys the sinner, the church, Christ's reputation, or other people generally. For instance, embezzlement does more damage than shoplifting, and murder does more damage than embezzlement.

danger or another, making the whole situation feel more urgent. There's the danger of public scandal and the damage that can be done to the reputation of Christ (1 Corinthians 5). There's the danger of division and the harm that can come to the church (Titus 3:10). There's the danger of false teaching and, again, the harm that can come to the church, especially weaker sheep (see 1 Tim. 1:20; 2 John 10–11). Now, a church should not move toward excommunication because of dangers alone, but the presence of danger indicates the seriousness of the sin and testifies to why the church should no longer affirm a profession of faith. That is to say, the danger (harm to Christ's reputation; threat of division or false teaching; harm to other sheep) must not be viewed as the *ground* of discipline, but it is a corroborating *witness* that affirms a swift act of discipline is the right course of action. It should also increase a church's sense of urgency, such that the necessary meetings and motions are called more quickly.

In short, the length of the process is determined entirely by how long it takes to convince the parties involved that a person is characteristically repentant or unrepentant. The church must examine the circumstances of the sin on one side of the balance, and all the other evidences of repentance on the other side. Sometimes new information will emerge that will tilt the scale in one direction or the other. But when the church is convinced that it has all the relevant information on both sides of the scale, and that the balance has stopped moving, it's called to act in the direction of whichever side is heavier. That process might take a minute, or it might take a year.

INDIVIDUALS SHOULD RECEIVE THE BENEFIT OF THE DOUBT

As we have already observed, Jesus prescribes something like a careful judicial process in Matthew 18: "that every charge may be established by the evidence of two or three witnesses" (v. 16). Charges must be established. Evidence must be presented. Witnesses must be involved. This means that Christians move slowly and carefully, but it also means that churches should approach discipline cases with something like the courtroom principle of "innocent until proven guilty."

This principle applies not only in matters of formal discipline, it also affects how a Christian should confront a brother or sister in private. People must be given the benefit of the doubt. Questions should precede accusations. Clarity should be sought before certainties are pronounced.

In the domain of discipline, as in every domain of life, "let every person be quick to hear, slow to speak, slow to anger" (James 1:19).

LEADERS SHOULD INVOLVE AND INSTRUCT THE CONGREGATION

Different denominational traditions have different ways of involving the entire congregation in the process of formal discipline. I personally recommend involving the congregation as a biblical principle, based on Matthew 18 (where Jesus involves "the church") and 1 Corinthians 5 (where Paul instructs the whole congregation to take responsibility). But for those yet unconvinced by the exegetical necessity, I still recommend looking for ways to involve the congregation as a theological and pastoral mandate. Theologically, Paul tells every part of the body to empathize with and own the experiences of every other part of the body, whether those parts are rejoicing or mourning (1 Cor. 12:21–26; see Eph. 4:16). Church discipline, particularly in its final stages, is a deeply significant event in the life of a body, which, by virtue of our shared union in Christ, every part surely *does* own. Pastorally, it's a significant event that every part surely *should* own. All will learn. All will be warned and challenged. All may have something to contribute.

In a congregational polity, the church will be asked to vote (in some contexts) or come to a consensus (in other contexts) on the final act of excommunication, an activity that appears to have a scriptural precedent. Notice the word "majority" in 2 Corinthians 2:6.

In other polities, the congregation might not be asked to become involved in the final decision to exclude a member, but the church leaders of every polity (I believe) should involve the congregation in at least four other ways. First, church leaders should "tell it to the church" before excluding someone (Matt. 18:17). Assuming a member is not in a situation requiring immediate removal, Jesus appears to envision a time lapse occurring between informing the church and the actual act of removal: "tell it to the church. And if he refuses to listen even to the church, let him be to you . . . " Presumably, this step gives church members who already have a relationship with the unrepentant individual the opportunity to pursue his or her repentance. Plus, it prepares the congregation for the final act of removal, should it occur. It gives them an opportunity to act and to ask questions before a final decision is announced.

Second, church leaders should tell the church after disciplining someone (if they have not included the church in the decision, which I think they should). The congregation should be informed of (if not involved in) the decision to exclude an individual. Scripture tells Christians that their relationships should markedly change with excluded individuals (as detailed in the next point); therefore, believers must be told of an individual's exclusion.

Third, church leaders should instruct and shepherd the congregation on how to view possible or actual acts of excommunication. Young Christians are often susceptible to naive and misplaced sympathies (as God sometimes said to the people of Israel). Leaders help keep them from stumbling by explaining the pertinent biblical texts and by modeling what a heartbroken, truth-loving compassion should look like.

Along these lines, leaders should also instruct members on how to interact with an individual who has been excluded. The New Testament addresses this matter in a number of places (1 Cor. 5:9, 11; 2 Thess. 3:6, 14–15; 2 Tim. 3:5; Titus 3:10; 2 John 10). The basic counsel the elders of my own church give is that the general tenor of one's relationships with the disciplined individual should markedly change. Interactions should not be characterized by casualness but by deliberate conversations about repentance. Certainly family members should continue to fulfill family obligations (see Eph. 6:1–3; 1 Tim. 5:8; 1 Pet. 3:1–2).

Fourth, leaders should lead congregations toward being prayerful and hopeful of repentance, ready to receive and be reconciled to the sinner. And such leadership occurs through careful instruction and personal example. There should be no doubt in anyone's mind that both the leaders and the church as a whole are heartbroken and want nothing more than to be reconciled with the estranged member.

ONE CHURCH'S APPROACH

Readers might have noticed that I have not provided a step-by-step outline for approaching a situation of church discipline. In part that's because Scripture offers several ways of approaching formal discipline. In part that's because different polities will prescribe different measures. In part that's because church leaders need to use wisdom for discerning which scriptural principles are relevant and applicable.

I can, however, explain how the process typically works in my own church. Broadly speaking, we follow the pattern set out in Matthew 18. Individuals have been taught to begin by addressing matters in private. If there is no private repentance, an elder or elders will become involved, first individually and eventually as a whole group. Sometimes the guilty party will meet with the elders as a whole, though individuals are not always willing to do this. The elders will then spend anywhere from a few days to a few months discussing whether to bring the matter to the congregation. If they decide to inform the congregation, they will present the pertinent information in a private meeting of members only. They will name the individual and designate the category of sin without providing too many details. The elders will explain any additional matters that are pertinent for pursuing the individual's repentance, and they will exhort the congregation to prayerfully pursue the member's repentance. They will explain that, if nothing changes in the situation, the elders will most likely move for excommunication at the next members' meeting, which would typically be two months away. Then the elders take questions from the members. Should the next members' meeting occur, and should the elders persist in their plan to exclude the individual, they will make a recommendation for excommunication, ask if there are any questions, and move for a vote among the members. If the members vote to excommunicate the individual, the elders then instruct the congregation on how to interact with the now-former member.

Whether the process plays out exactly like this, we always seek to implement the following principles:

1) The process should involve as few people as possible for yielding repentance.
2) When the process moves beyond one or several people, church leaders should lead the process.
3) The length of the process depends on how long it takes to establish that a person is characteristically unrepentant.
4) Individuals should receive the benefit of the doubt until the evidence indicates otherwise.
5) Leaders should involve and instruct the congregation as appropriate.

5

HOW DOES RESTORATION WORK?

If formal church discipline means removal from church membership and the Lord's Table, what is involved in restoration? And when does it occur? Those are the two questions we now consider: what and when.

WHAT IS RESTORATION?

After a person has been excommunicated from a church, restoration is simply the church declaring forgiveness toward the person and reaffirming his or her citizenship in God's kingdom.

In Paul's second letter to the Corinthian church, he addresses another case of church discipline, but this time he describes what restoration looks like. No details of the sin are provided, but the restoration is described this way:

> For such a one, this punishment by the majority is enough, so you should rather turn to forgive and comfort him, or he may be overwhelmed by excessive sorrow. So I beg you to reaffirm your love for him. (2 Cor. 2:6–8)

A majority of the congregation had deliberately acted (voted?) to punish the individual. Now Paul is telling them to forgive, to comfort, and to reaffirm their love for him.

The call to forgive the individual, moreover, is reminiscent of Jesus's words in John's Gospel, which parallel his words about the keys in Matthew's Gospel: "If you forgive the sins of any, they are forgiven them; if you withhold forgiveness from any, it is withheld" (John 20:23). Not long after this statement Jesus restored Peter (John 21:15–17).

Once a church decides to restore a repenting individual to its fellowship and the Lord's Table, there should be no talk of a probation period or second-class citizenship. Rather the church should publicly pronounce its forgiveness (John 20:23), affirm its love for the repenting individual (2 Cor. 2:8), and celebrate, just as the father of the Prodigal Son celebrated (Luke 15:24).

My own church once excommunicated an individual for a complicated situation involving a deep and unrepentant pattern of dishonesty. Gratefully, he eventually repented, and the church was able to pronounce its forgiveness and reaffirm its fellowship. Here is the motion that the elders put before the church:

Motion: The elders happily recommend that the members acknowledge with thankfulness to God the repentance of our brother, that we formally express to him our forgiveness for his actions toward us, and that we publicly renew our expression of fellowship with him and love for him as our brother in Christ. And we do all this with great thanks to God for his faithfulness to his Word and to those who honor it by their obedience.

The church unanimously affirmed it. It was an occasion for rejoicing.

Does restoration necessarily mean inclusion once more in the membership of the church? In most circumstances, I would say "yes." The repentance necessary for restoration will be indicated, among other things, by a willingness to reunite with a church and submit to its oversight. But ultimately I believe that restoration is analogous to baptism. Baptism ordinarily but not necessarily means inclusion into a church's membership (think of the Ethiopian eunuch in Acts 8:38–39). Restoration, in the same way, ordinarily but not necessarily means restoration into a church's membership. The individual in my example, in fact, was living in another country when the church voted on the above motion. He had e-mailed the church, confessed his sin, and asked what he could do to restore the relationship. After several exchanges, this motion was the conclusion of the matter.

WHEN SHOULD RESTORATION OCCUR?

When should restoration to a church occur? The simple answer is, when the sinner repents and the church is convinced the repentance is real because members see fruit in the individual's life. Restoration occurs when the church is willing to once more stand before the nations and vouch for the individual's profession of faith.

Sometimes the evidence of repentance is black and white: a man who has abandoned his wife returns. Sometimes the evidence will remain somewhat gray: a person caught in a cycle of addiction may not be completely victorious over the addiction, but there is much more victory now than there was in the past, and he has a new vigor in fighting it.

The necessary evidence for repentance will look different from sin to sin, and it will not always be easy to discern whether the repentance is real. The elders of my own church were once faced with a dilemma like this. An individual whom the church had disciplined was showing some evidence of repentance, but he also gave signs that his heart was still hard. As the elders deliberated about whether to recommend to the congregation the restoration of this man, we could all see both sides, and we all felt the weight of Paul's words about not letting the man be overwhelmed by excessive sorrow. In the final vote, seven voted against the restoration while six others voted for it.

It's possible, no doubt, that we as elders made a mistake, just as every decision a human or a church makes can be a mistake. But members of both the majority and the minority trusted God to be acting through our imperfect and somewhat divided deliberations. Gratefully, God uses tentative elder boards and fallible processes like our own.

Wisdom in assessing the evidence of repentance requires balancing caution with compassion. And this means the process must often proceed slowly—but not too slowly. In chapter 3 I related the story of a friend of mine who was excommunicated by his church for a shameful form of criminal activity. Gratefully, he immediately gave up the criminal activity once it was exposed—a good sign. But other related sins endured—a bad sign. He was willing to meet with two of the church's elders dozens of times for counseling—a good sign. But his attendance at church and counseling was sporadic—a bad sign. As of this writing, the pastors of the church are working to balance caution with compassion, to move slowly but not too slowly. The senior pastor of this church recently wrote me, "We remain hopeful the Lord will restore him yet! We had hoped that it would happen sooner, so as not to exasperate him. But we have not been able to move as fast as we would have liked. Please pray he will diligently seek the Lord."

As I said earlier, it would be nice to have a rule book for times like these: "When faced with *this*, do *that*." But it seems the Lord intends for his churches to learn what it means to trust the wisdom that he promises to give even in the toughest dilemmas, once again reminding us of how dependent we are upon him.

ARE OTHER CHURCHES BOUND?

There's one last question that's worth considering when it comes to discipline and restoration. Are other churches bound by a first church's decision to excommunicate an individual? That is, can one church receive as a member someone who has been disciplined by another church?

Different denominational traditions answer this question differently. Some traditions exist, in part, based on the conviction that the institutional church extends beyond the local church precisely so that this sort of thing does not happen. The actions of one bishop must be regarded as binding, in some measure, by another bishop.

But it's not just the Roman Catholics and the Anglicans for whom this is true. Some historical Baptists have argued that, when a church excommunicates an individual, the individual is still under the authority of that church, at least until it lifts the ban. In the meantime, another Baptist church must not usurp the first church's authority by receiving the individual as a member.

In my estimation, this argument is mistaken. Churches do have the authority to receive individuals disciplined by another congregation. They may not be wise to do so. And they would certainly be wise to investigate the action of the first church. But in the final analysis Jesus has given every congregation the authority of the keys for binding and loosing, and one congregation's decisions are not binding on another.

When a church excommunicates someone, it hands him over to Satan (1 Cor. 5:5). That is, it removes its affirmation that the individual belongs to God's kingdom, where God's redemptive authority rules. It declares instead that the person must belong to Satan's kingdom, where Satan rules (Matt. 4:8–9; John 12:31; 14:30). And the church has no more authority over the excommunicated member than it has over any other non-Christian in Satan's realm. Hence, Jesus says to treat them "as you would a pagan or a tax collector"

(Matt. 18:17, NIV)—someone who does not belong to God's covenant community.[3]

Am I recommending that churches act utterly autonomously from one another? Not at all. The churches of the New Testament are clearly interdependent. They see to it that other churches are provided for, receive good teaching, and work together for the truth (see Acts 11:28–30; Col. 4:16; 3 John 5–8). They also warn one another of false teachers and unsavory characters (1 John 4:1–3; 3 John 9–10). Part of such interdependence should include mutual help in receiving and dismissing members. Therefore, conversations between churches over matters of discipline, from time to time and within the bounds of prudence, should happen. But at the same time, every church is finally responsible before God to make its own decisions.

---

[3]But aren't churches to treat disciplined individuals differently than non-Christians (e.g., "With such a man do not even eat," 1 Cor. 5:11, NIV)? Yes. Isn't that a form of continuing authority? No. It's a form of authority exercised over the church's own members, as when a mother tells her children not to associate with a certain crowd at school. The authority is over the children, not over the wrong crowd. By telling its members not to associate with an excommunicated member, a church is both protecting its members and pronouncing that that individual's profession is fraudulent.

Part 2

APPLYING THE FRAMEWORK: CASE STUDIES

I have created the following "case studies" using elements of real-life situations that I have been involved with, or at least heard about. Even where I use real-life elements, I have altered the details in various ways, including the generic use of "Joe" and "Jill."

To avoid repetition and save space, I have left out detailed explanations, but instead refer the reader to the chapter in which I elaborate on the principle at play. The reference will appear parenthetically, as in (ch. 3) or (intr.).

I do not assume that the decisions made in what follows always represent the "final word." Some of them may be mistaken. Still, they represent either my church's or another church's best attempt at applying the gospel framework described in chapters 1 through 4.

Every scenario is described in the context of an elder-led, congregational model. That means the elders lead the process of discipline once it reaches a certain level, but the congregation has the final say in determining whether an excommunication should transpire, which is accomplished by voting, in a meeting of members only.

6

THE ADULTERER

SITUATION

Joe was actively involved in his church's benevolence ministry, even helping to lead it. His close friends, who were elders in the church, had begun to have conversations with Joe about his doubts concerning the Christian faith. One day Joe's wife contacted one of the elders and said that Joe had recently engaged in at least one extramarital affair, maybe more. Two elders met with him several times in private about both the adultery and the doubts, but to no avail. Joe admitted that his actions were "wrong," but his answers to questions about whether he would continue to see the other woman were evasive and unclear. Several weeks later, Joe told the two elders that he was leaving his wife and that he was done with the marriage. Within days, he moved out.

Should Joe be excommunicated? If so, how quickly?

ASSESSING THE SIN

Adultery is a grievous sin that immediately places a person's profession of faith in doubt. Some might say it undermines it completely. It's a significant act of betrayal that even non-Christians typically recognize as wrong, as testified to by the fact that politicians sometimes lose office if caught in adultery. Adultery deeply misrepresents Jesus, who has never been unfaithful to his bride. It destroys marriages, children, churches, and friendships.

In other words, adultery is not a sin that an individual stumbles into naively or unknowingly. It's a high-handed and deliberate sin that reveals a very hard and self-deceived heart.

It's not inconceivable that, in some circumstances, adultery might lead to immediate excommunication. This would be the case, for instance, if it quickly became apparent that there had been a pattern of such behavior, rather, say, than a one-night stand, or if it were immediately apparent that the individual was committed to continue pursuing the sin.

ASSESSING THE REPENTANCE

If an adulterer is caught, as Joe was, one might expect him to respond defensively, at least at first, even if he is a Christian. After all, a heart must have become pretty hard to go so far astray. Yet a Christian's heart should thaw fairly quickly when challenged over sexual immorality, probably within a matter of days if not hours. One should expect a repenting adulterer to be characterized, in Paul's words, by a godly and earnest grief, an eagerness to be done with the sin, indignation toward the sin, fear, longing, zeal, and more (2 Cor. 7:11).

From the beginning, however, Joe was evasive. It was not apparent that he meant to pursue the sin, but it was not apparent that he meant to give it up either. In the first couple of weeks, when only a couple of elders knew of the situation, Joe appeared to be in a state of indecision about which path he would choose. For this reason, they chose not to act immediately.

OTHER FACTORS

Joe's supposed doubts about the faith also played a factor in the elders' decision not to act immediately. He was even beginning to toy with the idea that he was not a Christian, which would have affected how they dealt with the situation (see the distinction Paul makes between associating with the sexually immoral in the world and the sexually immoral who bear "the name of brother," 1 Cor. 5:9–11). They assumed the doubts and the unfaithfulness were connected, but it wasn't clear which came first.

DECISION

As soon as Joe announced that he was leaving the marriage, and demonstrated his resolve by moving out, the elders determined that he was characteristically unrepentant (ch. 3). Joe had been warned repeatedly, but he was determined to pursue his sin rather than Jesus. He knew what he was doing. Therefore, the two elders moved, with the support of the entire elder board, for Joe's immediate excommunication (chs. 3 and 4). The church body assented.

7

THE ADDICT

SITUATION

Jill was addicted to gambling. She grew up in a home where her parents gambled recreationally and never with any great consequence. They even gave her a gambling allowance on family trips to Las Vegas. But in college, Jill's gambling became compulsive. She went to casinos. She joined several online fantasy leagues. She had gambling applications on her cell phone.

When Jill became a Christian after college, her gambling dramatically slowed down, mostly because she was distracted by her new faith. Then, over a year later, she began to gamble more often. At first her Christian friends, themselves somewhat immature, regarded her gambling stories as humorous. But not much time passed before they realized that she had a significant problem. One of them confronted Jill directly, and Jill agreed that gambling could be problematic if done irresponsibly, but she averred that hers was under control.

Then Jill married. Within a year, Jill's gambling was becoming the defining issue in the marriage. At first, she was defensive when her husband confronted her, pointing to his sin and to the fact that he had bet money on college basketball games when they were dating. But after one bad episode of losing a couple thousand dollars, she relented; she admitted that she had a gambling problem, and resolved to quit. Church friends were brought in for accountability.

Months passed. The accountability was vigorous at first, but then it slackened. Jill began to gamble again, and the problem escalated quickly. Her first time out, she risked high wagers, and lost a larger amount than she ever had before. The next day she tried to dig herself out of the hole by betting more, but fell deeper into it. A crash followed, involving both tears and renewed promises, even the promise to visit the church counselor. But in the ensuing months the cycle repeated itself several times.

Finally, one night, an elder received a phone call from Jill's husband: Jill was locked up after a drunken altercation with an off-duty police officer. She was at a casino, had lost thousands, felt horrible, sought refuge in alcohol, became belligerent, and eventually found herself swinging punches at the officer who had been trying to calm her down. He had not arrested her, but had placed her in the casino's "dry tank" and asked her husband to pick her up.

The next morning, Jill was deeply embarrassed, ostensibly remorseful, but also slightly defensive. It was embarrassing, yes, but part of her wanted to maintain that the sin wasn't *that* bad. That casinos had a dry tank was evidence, she reasoned, that her sin was fairly common. Besides, the officer let her off the hook; wouldn't her Christian friends do the same?

Should a church excommunicate an addict like Jill who

shows some signs of remorse over an addiction and its consequences?

ASSESSING THE SIN

Christians might disagree over whether small wagers of a dollar or two is sin. But most Christians would agree that betting larger amounts of money, particularly in a habitual fashion, is a sinfully poor stewardship of the resources God has given. More than likely, this kind of habit is driven by an idolatrous desire to get something for nothing. Further, such a habit most likely hinders a Christian from giving generously to one's church or to the needy. And surely it indicates a failure to love one's neighbor as oneself (who would encourage their neighbor to gamble large amounts of money?).

Jill's sin was clearly habitual and controlling. The feeling of risk was fun, but it also provided an escape from reality and it made her feel important (she admitted), as if winning bets demonstrated her mastery over chance and over the world. Clearly, she had developed an idol for the feelings of conquering risk as well as for getting something for nothing.

Equally if not more troubling was the fact that Jill sought refuge in drunkenness when idol number 1 failed her. Plus the public nature of her drunkenness and her violent behavior indicated that she had a complete lack of regard for her Christian witness and a fairly hardened heart.

ASSESSING THE REPENTANCE

By the time of the phone call, the discipline process had effectively been going on with Jill for years. The warnings had come. The accountability structures had been put in place. But Jill managed to forget about each structure. Sometimes she seemed repentant, but again and again she returned to her sin, like a dog to its vomit (Prov. 26:11). And each time, the problem seemed to get worse, like the demon who is exorcised only to return with seven brothers (Matt. 12:44–45).

Gratefully, Jill had intermittently determined to fight her sin, and she promised to do so after this most recent episode. She was certainly sorry the next day. But when the elders discussed the matter, it occurred to them that it would not take a regenerate heart to regret an evening of losing thousands of dollars, becoming inebriated, hitting a police officer, and getting locked up.

Three details seemed particularly problematic: the escalating nature of the gambling, what the most recent episode of public drunkenness and fighting revealed about the hardness of her heart, and the fact that her promises to change sounded a lot like promises everyone had heard before. One elder described the episode as "the last straw." And all the elders agreed that her words were no longer believable (chs. 3 and 4). All the "normal" accountability structures and pastoral counseling had not yielded fruit, and things were getting worse.

So little did even her husband trust her words of repentance at this point, that he told the elders he would support the decision to excommunicate his wife, not because he didn't love her, but because he did (intr.).

DECISION

The Sunday evening after the policeman's phone call the elders recommended excommunicating Jill immediately on the grounds of compulsive gambling and public drunkenness. It was the first time that many people in the church had heard about it, and some wondered whether a congregation-wide warning would have been best before actual excommunication. But the elders explained that the long pattern of events, punctuated by the fairly egregious character of her drunken altercation with a police officer, put the church in a position of being unable to affirm Jill's repentance with any integrity, at least for a period of time (ch. 3). Hopefully she would be able to demonstrate her repentance in the ensuing months, at which time they could happily and responsibly reaffirm her profession of faith (ch. 5).

Jill's husband made a deliberate point of attending the members' meeting. He wanted the congregation to know he supported the elders. He also wanted Jill to know that he stood with the church's decision, so that nothing might undermine the power that an act of excommunication would send to his wife.

The congregation voted to remove Jill with only one dissenting vote.

8

THE "HITS THE NEWS" LAWBREAKER

SITUATION

The elders and the congregation learned Tuesday morning from the local news that Joe had been arrested on charges of stealing from his company. Over the course of five years, the news report said, Joe had managed to steal several hundred thousand dollars. Joe pled not guilty, both before the court and in a private conversation with an elder.

Does the public nature of Joe's sin require the church to excommunicate him immediately?

ASSESSING THE SIN

To steal hundreds of thousands of dollars over several years while being a church member indicates deep settledness in one's sin and a deeply hardened and dishonest heart. Such sin is deliberate and high-handed.

ASSESSING THE REPENTANCE

In light of the sin's deliberateness, its duration, and its duplicitous nature, a church might reasonably decide that it is unable to affirm an individual's profession of faith, and therefore move for immediate excommunication. Such an individual *could* be repentant, but a church would have a hard time determining whether someone truly was. More likely, the sin of embezzlement and the accompanying duplicity would point to characteristic unrepentance (chs. 3 and 4).

But this analysis presumes that Joe was guilty, and he pled not guilty. Plus the court had not yet decided. The elders didn't want the church's judicial decision to be less informed than the court's (ch. 1). And they certainly didn't want to excommunicate a man that the court might eventually exonerate.

DECISION

Since the congregation already knew about the situation from the newspapers, the elders knew that they would need to say something to the church. Therefore, the elders agreed:

1) to wait for the court's decision before making a formal recommendation;
2) to tell the congregation that this was their course of action;
3) to call the congregation to pray and show love for Joe and his family in the meantime;
4) and they also privately encouraged Joe to continue attending the Lord's Day gatherings, but, if he knew himself to be guilty, to abstain from the Lord's Supper. They assumed that, if guilty, he would ignore this advice. But they still needed to discharge it.

9

THE BRUISED REED

SITUATION

Jill was raised by a single mom who had multiple partners, several of whom had treated her and Jill abusively. Longing for a steady male figure, Jill, too, established a pattern in early adolescence of sleeping around and letting herself be taken advantage of by men. She also developed patterns of self-cutting and bulimia.

In college, Jill found friends in a church college group who seemed to care about her. Somewhere along the way she started calling herself a Christian and was baptized. Her church preached the gospel, but most of the preaching was shallow, and the church offered little in the way of accountability. Most attendees, including Jill, remained anonymous. Jill soon fell back into her old patterns of sexual sin and self-cutting.

After college, she began attending a new church where the Bible was faithfully taught and membership was emphasized. She joined. She mostly remained on the periphery of the new church, but she did join a small group with other women where, in time, she found herself admitting how lonely she was and, somewhat to her own surprise, confessing her sexual sin.

One day, she arrived at the pastor's office along with a supportive small group member, and she confessed through tears to an alarming level of sexual activity over the period of several months.

Should Jill be excommunicated? Should the circumstances of her background weigh into the decision?

ASSESSING THE SIN

In general, fornication calls into question a Christian's profession of faith, particularly when the fornication has been a pattern or a lifestyle, as it had been with Jill. In her early days as a Christian, she vaguely knew that it was wrong, but her church did not seem to take sin seriously. The college leader made the occasional risqué joke, and other members of the college group were known to fool around. She used these things as excuses to harden her own conscience.

In the new church, however, her sense of hypocrisy and conviction grew. Yet the sexual patterns and emotional needs were deep. The self-cutting provided a temporary sense of absolution over the guilt of sexual sin.

ASSESSING THE REPENTANCE

As troubling as Jill's pattern of sin was, her first steps of repentance were encouraging (ch. 3). First, she brought the sin into the light herself; she had not been caught. Second, she had told her small group and then, at great embarrassment to herself, a pastor whom she only knew by acquaintance and whom she respected from a distance. Third, she agreed at his request to meet with a staff counselor in the church. Fourth, she said she would prefer for him not to tell the elders, but would respect his decision to do so, knowing that he would act for her good. Through all of this, there was no defensiveness in Jill (ch. 3). She seemed to genuinely mourn the past and long for a different kind of future.

The self-cutting was problematic in that it displayed a weak grasp on the gospel. Still, her determination to bring both the cutting and the sexual sin into the light no matter the cost to herself spoke well of her repentance.

OTHER FACTORS

Jill's family background played heavily in how the pastor assessed this situation. Had a woman who had grown up in the church and in a healthy family and who had been active in church ministry confessed to this level of sin, his assessment might have been different.

DECISION

The pastor decided to present the situation to the entire elder board, but to not recommend excommunication. He shared Jill's story both to check his own response, but also so that the elders would better know how to care for this bruised reed. No formal action was taken.

10

THE NONATTENDING MEMBER

SITUATION

Joe joined the church in January, attended somewhat inconsistently for six months, and then stopped coming altogether. During the time he did attend, he arrived at church late, left early, and never made any relationships. One elder managed to have lunch with him in February, and attempted to schedule further meals. But Joe canceled each one at the last minute, usually because, "Something just came up at work. Sorry!" No one else in the church seemed to know Joe.

In September, the elder realized he had not seen Joe at church since June, and decided to call him again. He left a voicemail. A few weeks later, he left another voicemail, along with an e-mail. None of his messages were returned. Several more months passed with no sight or sound of Joe. One or two more messages had been left. At this point, the elder explained the situation to the other elders, two of whom offered to call or e-mail Joe. Several elders' meetings later, Joe's name came up again, and everyone agreed that they had not seen or heard from him in over eight months.

Should Joe be excommunicated? If so, for what sin?

ASSESSING THE SIN

Joe's sin could be described in several ways. He could be characterized as violating his church covenant in which he promised to take responsibility for this local church. He could be characterized as claiming to love God while also hating his brothers and sisters in the church by utterly neglecting them (1 John 4:20–21). Perhaps most concretely, Joe was disobeying the command of Hebrews 10:24–25, which reads, "And let us consider how to stir up one another to love and good works, not neglecting to meet together, as is the habit of some, but encouraging one another, and all the more as you see the Day drawing near." The author of Hebrews commands Christians to meet regularly so that they can encourage one another and provoke one another to love and good deeds, which is another way of making the first two points above. The author then points to the day of judgment as incentive for why this must be done. In other words, he takes this sin very seriously, indeed.

The sin of nonattendance is not nearly as obvious as something like adultery. Nonetheless, it's a sin that's often hiding other sin, or at least leading to other sin. Plus, nations like the United States are filled with nominal Christians who bring ill-repute to the gospel because churches have not taken responsibility for their nonattenders.

Further, if church membership consists in the church's public affirmation of an individual's profession of faith, nonattendance renders the church incapable of fulfilling its responsibility. The church can no longer claim with integrity to oversee one's discipleship. Therefore, excommunication effectively sets the record straight. It's the church's way of saying, "We cannot account for this individual. Therefore we are no longer going to formally affirm his profession of faith" (ch. 2).

ASSESSING THE REPENTANCE
Since Joe refused to respond to the elders' e-mails and phone calls, there was no way to measure the fruit of repentance, other than to say that there was none.

DECISION
Still, the elders decided not to move toward immediate excommunication. Instead, they decided to "tell it to the church," to use the language of Matthew 18 (ch. 1). At the next members' meeting, therefore, they put Joe's name in front of the congregation and explained that, if nothing changed, they would move for excommunication on the grounds of nonattendance at the next regularly scheduled meeting in two months' time. They encouraged anyone who had a relationship with Joe to call or e-mail him. The elders also used the opportunity to teach the congregation why attendance is so important.

They delayed the motion for excommunication by two more months for at least five reasons (ch. 4). First, it gave more time, in accordance with the logic of Matthew 18, to test for Joe's repentance. Second, it gave Joe's friends—in case he had any that the elders were unaware of—the opportunity to join them in the work of calling Joe to repentance. Third, it would take away the shock factor that inevitably attends motions for immediate excommunication. Satan often uses this shock to undermine any confidence that younger and immature sheep have in their leaders. Fourth, it was a last-resort measure for tracking down this strayed sheep. Fifth, it gave the congregation an opportunity to pray together for Joe.

Two months later, no one had heard anything from Joe. The elders therefore moved for excommunication, and the congregation unanimously assented.

11

THE FAITHFULLY-ATTENDING AND DIVISIVE NONMEMBER

SITUATION

Jill and her husband had been attending their church for twenty years. For most of that time, the church did not formally practice membership, and neither Jill nor her husband had ever joined. Still, both were actively involved in everything from organizing meals for new mothers to teaching Sunday school. And they seldom missed a Sunday.

Jill was also an active gossip. She always seemed to be the first to know about one couple's marital difficulties, another's financial troubles, and still another's difficulty with rebellious teenagers.

When a new pastor arrived and began to implement a more careful regimen of meaningful church membership, most of the church happily assented. Jill and her husband, however, did not. They resented the idea of being made to sign anything pertaining to their Christianity. They argued that "the church is a family!" and "who would make family members sign a form saying they were part of a family?"

Over several years, the new pastor made a number of other changes that Jill and her husband did not like, such as implementing a policy that only members could teach Sunday school or lead in other ministries, like church-sponsored hospitality. The couple grew in resentment, especially Jill.

One day, Jill saw the pastor in a back aisle of the grocery store speaking with an attractive young woman who was not his wife. Jill was standing at a distance, but she thought she saw him touch the woman's shoulder, and that the woman either cried or giggled in response. She wasn't sure. But she began to tell her friends that she was concerned for the pastor, that he might be having an affair, and that he needed prayer. This rumor began to spread, and word eventually reached the elders.

At first, Jill would not directly address the matter with the pastor or the other elders. But when two elders told her to stop gossiping and to apologize to her friends, she decided to formally confront the pastor and his wife. By then Jill had talked herself into believing that he was indeed having an affair. The elders asked if she could bring another witness to corroborate her charge (1 Tim. 5:19). She could not, yet she refused to relent. When the elders warned Jill about the possibility of excommunication for slander and for divisiveness, she said that they did not have the authority to excommunicate her since she was not a member.

Can a church excommunicate a nonmember? What are the criteria for determining when one's slander and divisiveness have crossed the line and become actionable?

ASSESSING THE SIN

Based on the evidence, Jill appeared to be culpable for at least three sins: slander, divisiveness, and refusing to submit to the elders. Jesus and the apostles characterize slander as evil and require Christians to put it away (Matt. 15:19; Eph. 4:31; 1 Pet. 2:1). After all, it can destroy the reputation and possibly the livelihood of a Christian brother or sister, and it produces disunity in the church. Paul also warns that those who cause division should be warned twice and then excluded (Titus 3:10). Divisiveness is taken very seriously, indeed. Finally, Scripture enjoins Christians to submit to their leaders (Heb. 13:17).

Jill's charges were based on the incident in the grocery store and one or two other random details of no account. Still, two elders quietly investigated but found the charges utterly fanciful. They asked her to stop making accusations on at least four occasions, but she refused.

ASSESSING THE REPENTANCE

After six to eight weeks of conversations, it became clear that Jill would not relent. In fact, she seemed to harden in her position with every conversation, and began to embellish her description of what she witnessed at the grocery store. Friends who were originally sympathetic with her concerns started backing away from her. This seemed to enrage her further and caused her to turn to younger, more immature members in the search for allies.

In short, Jill's years of involvement and ministry in the church argued that Jill was a Christian. But the most recent months seemed to undermine this (ch. 3). The elders unanimously agreed she was committing all three sins described above, and for these there was absolutely no evidence of repentance. The fruit was bad and was getting worse.

OTHER FACTORS

The complicating factor in this situation was that Jill was not a member of the church. Technically, she was correct: she had never formally submitted to the authority of the congregation, and so the church did not have the formal authority to excommunicate her (chs. 2 and 3).

At the same time, she was well-known and liked by a majority of the congregation due to her long experience in the church. Plus, many people simply assumed that she was a member. Some even felt indebted to her for the way she had cared for them, such as the young mothers for whom she had provided meals. In a sense, she was everything a member is supposed to be, apart from her sin. The combination of attendance, relationships, and receiving the Lord's Supper testified to insiders and outsiders alike that the church affirmed her profession of faith.

DECISION

Slander and divisiveness can be hard to measure, but the elders determined to treat her actions as such since they met several criteria:

- She was making claims that she could not corroborate with either evidence or another witness.
- She refused to cease making accusations when asked to stop.

- She was tempting other members to question, suspect, and even criticize the leadership.
- She was actively recruiting fellow dissenters.
- Her activity had become a palpable distraction in the church's life. It frequently arose in conversations between members. It consumed elder time. And members admitted that it affected their ability to listen to sermons.

The elders therefore determined that this woman was a wolf, and that the Bible clearly instructs shepherds to warn the flock against wolves—members or not (Acts 20:28–31; see 2 Peter 2; Rev. 2:20–29). Therefore, they privately instructed her to abstain from the Lord's Supper until she publicly repented, and they warned the congregation of her slander and divisiveness in a meeting of members. They also told the church not to treat her like a Christian, and to avoid being duped by her misleading and destructive ways.

Since she was not a member, the elders decided not to call for any action by the congregation, nor would they use the word "excommunication" (ch. 2). Instead, they told the congregation that the elders' actions should be construed as activities of instruction and warning, which they had the authority to do by virtue of what it means to be an overseer (Acts 20:28–31).

12

THE PREEMPTIVE RESIGNER

SITUATION

Joe decided to divorce his wife after twenty years of marriage. He had done well for himself financially, and his purchases increasingly reflected that fact. When challenged about the divorce, he claimed that he and his wife had "grown irrevocably apart" and "were just occupying a common residence." Joe's wife sadly agreed with this assessment, but didn't want the divorce.

Several of Joe's friends begged him to stop pursuing this course of action. Eventually they involved one of the pastors, who used the words "church discipline" in the course of the forty-five-minute meeting. One week later, Joe sent a letter of resignation to the church office. He simultaneously submitted all the paperwork necessary for the divorce.

Should Joe be excommunicated? Can a church member avoid church discipline by resigning his or her membership?

ASSESSING THE SIN

Christians disagree about whether Jesus and Paul permitted divorce for matters such as unfaithfulness and abandonment (see Matt. 19:9; 1 Cor. 7:15), but most Christians agree that a Christian cannot legitimately divorce a spouse for the reasons Joe provided. Such an action would be a violation of the marriage covenant established by God and is therefore a sin.

Further, such a sin, particularly when pursued in the face of several warnings, would be clear, deliberate, and high-handed. It would seem to immediately discredit one's profession of faith.

ASSESSING THE REPENTANCE

Repentance in such an instance would be fairly black-and-white: stop pursuing the divorce. Yet Joe showed no signs of turning away from his course of action.

OTHER FACTORS

Joe attempted to avoid excommunication by resigning his membership. Was this legitimate? No. Christians are called, as a matter of obedience to Christ, to submit to the affirmation and oversight of local churches (ch. 2). People join churches by the consent of the church, and they resign by the consent of the church. That is to say, a person cannot walk up to a church and say, "I'm a member now." Churches of every polity have some way of testing and then affirming a person's profession of faith. Jesus gave the apostolic church the keys of the kingdom for this very purpose. Yes, church membership is "voluntary" insofar as Jesus does not bind us to choose one church rather than another, but he does bind us to choosing *some* church. And just as a person cannot "member" himself, he cannot "unmember" himself. Church members cannot simply preempt a church's threat of discipline with a resignation (ch. 2); the end of this covenant-like relationship requires the consent of both parties.[4] Permitting such an action would undermine Jesus's very purpose in giving local churches the keys of the kingdom for exercising discipline. It would be equivalent to letting an arrested criminal resign his citizenship in order to avoid prosecution and conviction.

DECISION

The elders determined that they would not ask the church to act on his resignation. Instead they asked the church to excommunicate Joe on the grounds of divorce. Since Joe's actions, after multiple warnings, were indicative of characteristic unrepentance, and since the movement toward divorce was now a settled and legal fact, they asked the congregation to excommunicate Joe immediately (chs. 3 and 4). The congregation agreed and voted to exclude Joe from membership and the Lord's Table.

---

[4]For a longer discussion on this point, see my article "The Preemptive Resignation—A Get Out of Jail Free Card?" at 9Marks, November/December 2009, http://www.9marks.org/ejournal/preemptive-resignation-get-out-jail-free-card.

13

THE NEWLY DECIDED UNBELIEVER

SITUATION

Jill grew up in a nonreligious household. In college she majored in philosophy and described herself as an agnostic. Then she became a deist. Then she briefly flirted with Zen Buddhism. Then she began dating a Christian and decided to become a Christian. After college the couple married and joined a church.

Five years into the marriage, Jill began to question her faith and ultimately decided that, even if Jesus existed as a historical figure, he certainly did not rise from the dead. After several meetings with an elder to discuss her doubts, she decided it was best to renounce the faith, resign her church membership, and stop calling herself a Christian.

Should a church excommunicate someone who no longer professes to be a Christian?

DECISION

Once Jill made her decision, the pastor warned her and urged her to repent, but he did not recommend excommunication to the other elders, nor did the elders recommend it to the congregation. Instead, they announced that Jill had renounced the faith and was calling herself an unbeliever, and that they were removing her name from the membership list, not as an act of excommunication, but according to her request.

Their rationale: Jesus has given local churches authority over Christians, not over non-Christians (ch. 2). Hence, the church had no real authority to act here. Further, Paul said the church's judgment pertained to "anyone who bears the name of brother" (1 Cor. 5:11), and she no longer did.

Certainly many situations of significant doctrinal deviation and apostasy would call for excommunication, as Paul explains to Timothy (1 Tim. 1:18–20). And surely the eternal effects of Jill's decision are no less terrible than what Paul foresees for those who deny the "faith and a good conscience," thereby shipwrecking their faith (v. 19). Still, the situation Paul addresses with Timothy involved active blasphemy (v. 20), which, almost by definition, involves the attempt to actively mislead church members. And Jill's situation was not like this.

The elders therefore said there was no action to be taken on the part of the congregation, just as there is no action to be taken when a member dies. In both cases, the membership, as it were, vanishes. They did instruct the congregation to pursue Jill in friendship, to treat her like any other non-Christian by welcoming her into their homes, and to evangelize her.

14

THE FAMILY MEMBER

SITUATION

Joe's wife was recently excommunicated for her addiction to gambling (see chap. 7's case study). Joe agreed with the church's decision. But after the decision, he read his Bible and discovered that Paul says "not even to eat with such a one" (1 Cor. 5:11).

Joe's wife was deeply upset by the church's decision and felt spurned by his decision to vote with the congregation. But she had no plans of leaving him, and he had no plans of leaving her (see 1 Cor. 7:12–14). Yet now he wondered whether he should avoid eating with her altogether.

How should a family member treat an individual who has been excommunicated?

DECISION

In a private meeting, an elder explained to Joe that he was still scripturally obligated to love, serve, and care for his wife, even laying down his life for her as Christ did for the church (see 1 Cor. 7:14–15; Eph. 5:25–30). The elder distinguished the creation and common grace institution of marriage from the redemptive and special grace institution of the local church.

The fact that Joe's wife had been excommunicated from the church did not abrogate his marital responsibilities.

In general, the elder explained, the family members of a disciplined individual should continue to fulfill the biblical obligations of family life (e.g., Eph. 6:1–3; 1 Tim. 5:8). And surely this would include the duty of children *to eat* with their parents, or husbands with their wives.

Still, the church's act of excommunication meant that a new burden was placed on Joe and how he was to interact with his wife. Paul's purpose in charging church members not to eat with excommunicated members served at least three purposes: to protect Christians from the leaven of sin; to protect excluded members from thinking the church regarded them as believers; and to protect the church's witness in the community. In the days of the early church, sharing a meal with an individual communicated the extension of fellowship, care, and protection (hence, the religious leaders objected to Jesus's eating with sinners and tax collectors). And Paul did not want church members to engage with excommunicated members *in any way* that would communicate this kind of shared Christian fellowship.

By this token, Joe would need to strike the balance of simultaneously affirming his love for his wife, even romantically, and serving her to the utmost, while also making sure that he did not say or do anything that would make her think that he thought she was a Christian. Instead, he would need to continue encouraging her toward repentance and faith.

Part 3

GETTING STARTED

15

BEFORE YOU DISCIPLINE, TEACH

Mark Dever, an experienced pastor and a well-known advocate of church discipline, begins an article on the topic of church discipline with these unexpected words: "'Don't do it.' That's the first thing I tell pastors when they discover church discipline is in the Bible. I say, 'Don't do it, at least not yet.'"[5]

Why would someone who calls church discipline one of the marks of a healthy church begin with this advice? Dever envisions a pastor hearing about discipline for the first time. At first, the idea sounds ridiculous to this pastor. But then he looks at all the scriptural texts, and conviction settles in. He realizes that he's been careless. He's not been guarding the church or the reputation of Christ. He's not been loving his sheep or their non-Christian neighbors. Conviction turns to resolve, and the imaginary pastor determines to press forward. Dever continues:

---

[5]Mark Dever, "Don't Do It!! Why You Shouldn't Practice Church Discipline," at 9Marks, November/December 2009, www.9marks.org/eJournal/don't-do-it-why-you-shouldnt -practice-church-discipline.

It's at this point that a sullen resolve often seems to set in. "I will lead this congregation to be biblical at this point if it's the last thing I do!" And, too often, it is.

Into the peaceful, well-meaning life of an innocent, Bible-believing congregation, the lightning bolt of church discipline strikes! It may be in a sermon. It may be in a conversation between the pastor and a deacon. It may be in a hastily arranged motion at a members meeting. But somewhere it hits, usually accompanied by great earnestness and a torrent of Scriptural citations.

Then, the sincere action is taken.

Then, the response comes: misunderstanding and hurt feelings result. Counter charges are made. Sin is attacked and defended. Names are called. Acrimony abounds! The symphony of the local congregation transposes into a cacophony of arguments and accusations. People cry out, "Where will this stop?!" and "So do you think you're perfect?"[6]

The moral of the story, of course, is that a number of preparatory steps need to be taken before pastors push toward practicing formal church discipline. In this chapter we'll consider what pastors need to teach. In the next chapter we'll consider some organizational matters that are good to get in place.

TEACH ABOUT HOLINESS AND REPENTANCE

If the idea of church discipline is to make any sense to a church at all, a congregation must have a robust understanding of the gospel and what it means to be a Christian, as we discussed in the preface and chapter 2. Being a Christian is

[6]Ibid.

not just about making a one-time decision; it's about a faith and repentance that yield a whole new pattern of decisions. It's about submitting to Christ as Lord.

God intends for his people to look different than the world. He intends for them to live holy lives and to war against sin. That's what it means to repent. Repentance does not mean that a person has stopped sinning, but it does mean that he has declared war against sin. A congregation must understand these things before one can expect it to understand church discipline.

TEACH ABOUT MEMBERSHIP

A church won't be willing to put someone *out* of the church unless they understand that there is an *in* and an *out*. The Bible is clear: there are those who are "members" of the body of Christ (1 Cor. 12:27) and those who are "outsiders" (1 Cor. 5:12). If a congregation does not understand this, the idea of putting someone "out" will sound quite ridiculous.

More specifically, a church needs to understand that church membership is not like membership in a club or some other voluntary organization. It's about citizenship in a kingdom in which we are affirmed and recognized as ambassadors by the king's embassy-like representative, the local church. Individual Christians do not have the authority, once they become convinced that they are Christians, to stand before the world and say, "Hey world, I'm with Jesus," through self-baptism and giving themselves the Lord's Supper. No, the church has that authority, through the power of the keys.

What is church membership? Church membership is the church's public affirmation of an individual Christian's profession of faith in Jesus, and it's the individual's decision to submit to the oversight of the church. When your church begins to understand that, the idea of church discipline will start to make a lot more sense.

It will also help people to understand why they don't have the authority to simply resign their membership when threatened with discipline. People join a church by the authority of a church, and they exit a church by the authority of a church.

TEACH ABOUT DISCIPLESHIP

As we saw in the early chapters, discipleship and discipline involve both teaching and correcting. And this discipleship will occur both privately and corporately.

Congregations need to understand therefore that part of being a disciple of Christ is knowing how to be corrected and taught by other disciples of Christ. Pastors need to encourage church members to build relationships with one another in which correction and instruction are normal. They should teach them that a gospel-grounded individual learns how to invite correction, and how to tenderly give it. Older men with younger men. Older women with younger women.

When this kind of accountability typifies the personal relationships in a church, formal church discipline makes more sense. When it doesn't, the proposal to move toward a formal act of discipline will feel like it's coming out of nowhere.

TEACH ABOUT SELF-DECEPTION

Discipleship exists in part because people, including Christians, are prone to self-deception. That's why the apostles again and again warn Christians not to "be deceived" (1 Cor. 6:9; Gal. 6:7; James 1:16). "Let no one deceive himself," Paul says (1 Cor. 3:18). And elsewhere: "evil people and impostors will go on from bad to worse, deceiving and being deceived" (2 Tim. 3:13). It's easy to say we have no sin and so "deceive ourselves," John says (1 John 1:8). Even our very desires are "deceitful" (Eph. 4:22).

Christians who forget that they are prone to self-deception have already become proud, and they're on the fast track to self-righteous Phariseeism. The solution: invite discipline. Ask for correction. Welcome rebuke. This is the way of humility and wisdom.

Local churches exist, in part, to protect us from ourselves. It's the brothers and sisters around us who love us and are committed to our good that help us to see the things we cannot see about ourselves. We are not the world's experts on "us."

This is a lesson pastors should teach week after week in the good times, so that when rebellious times come, the church is ready for it.

TEACH ABOUT DISCIPLINE

The congregation needs to be taught about church discipline through the most prominent texts on the topic, such as Matthew 18 and 1 Corinthians 5. Sermons, small groups, and church newsletters are all natural forums for this kind of instruction.

But pastors should also learn how to apply other passages of Scripture to the topics of membership and discipline (where appropriate). For instance, the passage on being holy because God is holy in 1 Peter has clear individual applications, but it also has corporate applications: If God's *people* should be holy, we as a church should exercise care in who we receive and dismiss as church members.

Or consider the passages in John's Gospel and epistles about love leading to obedience. Such passages have not only personal but corporate applications: How do we learn to love one another better in our church? By helping one another to obey and by sensitively correcting one another when we don't. To correct a disobedient brother in Christ, when done with the right motives, is an act of love. Do you believe that?

In fact, just about any text in the Bible on holiness, repentance, conversion, lordship, and discipleship, not to mention texts touching on the broad themes of redemptive history such as Israel's boundary markers or exile, can easily be applied in the direction of discipline.

Pastors should also teach church members about the purposes of discipline. Churches must not practice discipline for the sake of retribution, but for the sake of gospel love. We saw in chapter 1 that discipline serves to expose cancerous sin, to warn against a greater judgment, to save the sinner, to protect other church members, and to present a good witness for Christ—all of which are activities of love.

TEACH ABOUT LOVE

Church discipline, then, is fundamentally about love. The Lord disciplines those he loves (Heb. 12:6). The same is true for his church.

The problem is, most people today have a sentimentalized view of love: love as being made to feel special. Or they have a romanticized view of love: love as being allowed to express yourself without judgment. Or they have a consumeristic view: love as finding the perfect fit for you. In the popular mind, love has little to do with truth and holiness and authority.

But that's not love in the Bible. Love in the Bible is holy. It makes demands. It yields obedience. It doesn't delight in evil but rejoices in the truth (1 Cor. 13:6).

Jesus tells us that if we keep his commandments, we will abide in his love (John 15:10). And John tells us that if we keep the word of Christ, God's love will be perfected in us (1 John 2:5). How do church members help one another abide in Christ's love and see to the perfection of God's love in one another? Through helping one another obey and keep his word. Through instruction and correction.

A church that understands biblical love stands a far better chance of understanding church discipline.

16

BEFORE YOU DISCIPLINE, ORGANIZE

Preparing a church to practice church discipline often involves more than teaching. It also might require some organizational change. Let me point to four organizational matters.

GET THE CHURCH'S DOCUMENTS IN PLACE

Some churches have bylaws. Some have constitutions. Some have statements of faith and church covenants. Whatever a church might have, churches in Western contexts will serve their members by making sure the documents explain (1) what's expected of members in terms of belief and behavior; (2) how the church's authority structures operate; (3) what to expect for the receiving and dismissing of members under ordinary circumstances; (4) how church discipline works for the extraordinary circumstances.

It's an act of kindness to let people know what standards they are going to be held accountable to before you discipline them. A statement of faith lets them know what they are expected to believe. A covenant lets them know how they are expected to live. A constitution lets them know how member-ship and discipline work.

Such documents also promote unity. Agreed-upon docu-ments spare the church from controversies over the methods or rules every time a disagreement arises.

ENSURE PROPER LEGAL FOUNDATIONS

Getting a church's documents in place also helps to establish the proper legal foundations for practicing church discipline in a highly litigious society. Churches have been successfully sued over church discipline.[7]

One of the most effective ways to prevent such lawsuits is to adopt explicit biblical policies that comprehensively describe how your church will exercise discipline over unre-pentant members. And one of the most effective defenses to any lawsuit is informed consent. To secure this defense, a church needs to be able to prove to a court that the person complaining of a wrong was in fact fully aware of the church's policies and procedures and knowingly agreed to be bound by them.

In addition to making discipline procedures explicit in a church's constitution or bylaws, a church should explic-itly teach its discipline procedures in church membership classes.

An excellent resource on these matters is Peacemaker Ministries: www.peacemaker.net.

---

[7]See Ken Sande's article, "Informed Consent: Biblical and Legal Protection for Church Discipline," 9Marks, September/October 2009, http://www.9marks.org/ejournal/informed-consent-biblical-and-legal-protection-church-discipline.

ORGANIZE THE CHURCH'S MEMBERSHIP ROLLS

Practicing church discipline requires churches to know *who the church is*. Several years back, a friend of mine accepted the position of senior pastor at an international church in the Middle East. When he got there, six hundred people were in attendance, but no real membership rolls had been kept. There was an old phone directory with some one hundred names and nothing more. He summarized the situation for me like this: "We didn't know who we were." Neither he nor anyone else in the church knew who had agreed to be held accountable by the body. The church had been faithful to preach. It had not been faithful in its work of exercising the keys through baptism, the Lord's Supper, or church discipline.

What if my friend had attempted to bring a case of discipline before the church at that point? The process would have broken down at multiple points: the individual being charged could claim that he was not under the church's authority; other church leaders might agree; and other attenders wouldn't know if they were to participate in making the decision or not.

Other churches have a different problem than my friend in the Middle East. They have formal membership rolls that far exceed the attendance—three hundred in attendance; one thousand on the rolls. When that's the case, it's difficult to exercise discipline with integrity. How can a church discipline one individual for nonattendance while leaving the 699 alone?

In short, church leaders, in most circumstances, need to organize their church's membership rolls before practicing discipline. The list of members needs to consist mostly of people who are present at the church's weekly gatherings (of course there are exceptions for shut-ins, members of the military on a temporary tour of duty, etc.).[8]

ENSURING THE LEADERS AGREE

Finally, it's important to make sure that a church's leadership as a whole is on board with church discipline, both in principle and in any given instance of practice. If one pastor or elder leads the charge while the others sit back, because they are doubtful of either the principle or the particular application, disunity in the church will result. Therefore, if a pastor must teach the entire church about discipline, as we discussed in the last chapter, he certainly needs to make sure he has taught his fellow leaders.

Moving forward on church discipline can produce volatile discussions. For such occasions, a man surely wants to stand shoulder to shoulder with mature leadership who share his convictions.

---

[8]For guidance on how to do this, see Matt Schmucker's two articles, "Cleaning Up the Rolls" and "Cleaning Up the Rolls (Part 2): The Care List," 9Marks, http://www.9marks.org/ejournal/cleaning-rolls and http://www.9marks.org/ejournal/cleaning-rolls-part-2-care-list. See also Mark Dever's "Why We Disciplined Half Our Church," LeadershipJournal.net, Oct. 1, 2000, http://www.christianitytoday.com/le/2000/fall/16.101.html.

CONCLUSION

Are You Ready to Begin? A Pastor's Checklist

When pastors of churches that are unknown to me ask whether they should proceed with discipline, I will ask them about the details of the situation itself. But I will also walk them through a checklist that looks a lot like the subheadings from the last two chapters. Over the phone or in person, I typically run through questions like these:

A PASTOR'S CHECKLIST FOR CHURCH DISCIPLINE

Teaching

1) Does your congregation have an understanding of the gospel that includes repentance, obedience, and the lordship of Christ?

2) Does your church practice careful membership? Does your congregation understand the church's authority and the call to help one another remain accountable in the faith? Do church members practice such accountability privately?

3) Do they understand that Christian discipleship includes both instruction and correction?

4) Do they understand that they are prone to self-deceit, and that God has lovingly and wisely placed other Christians in their lives for this very purpose?

5) Have you taught the church about church discipline? Once, or on numerous occasions? Have other teachers had the opportunity to teach about it as well, whether in Sunday school classes or small groups? Does the church seem to embrace it as being biblical?

Structure

6) Do your church documents reflect the practice of discipline? Have members been taught to expect discipline when joining the church? Have they been taught to approach an elder if they change their minds on some matter in the statement of faith? Do they know they will be held accountable for living according to scriptural principles?

7) That is, does your church have proper legal foundations—can you establish informed consent?

8) Do your membership rolls reflect who you are preaching to on Sunday?

9) Do your fellow leaders understand discipline, agree with it, and perceive its importance?

The Specific Situation

10) If this is the first time the church has practiced discipline, is the case a comparatively simple case? That is, is the sin in question one that you expect the whole church will agree is gravely out of sync with a person who is a representative of Jesus?

APPENDIX

Mistakes Pastors Make in Practicing Discipline

Pastors sometimes make the following mistakes regarding formal church discipline.

1) They fail to teach their congregation what church discipline is and why they should practice it.

2) They fail to practice meaningful membership, which includes (1) teaching people what membership entails before they join; (2) encouraging casual attenders to join; (3) carefully interviewing everyone who wants to join; (4) giving regular oversight to all the flock; and (5) maintaining an up-to-date membership list that accurately reflects who is present at the weekly gathering.

3) They fail to teach their congregation about biblical conversion, especially the need for repentance.

4) They fail to teach new members as they enter the church about the possibility of church discipline, and that preemptive resignations don't work.

5) They fail to ensure that the church's public documents (bylaws, constitution, articles of incorporation, etc.) address the procedures of church discipline, thereby exposing the church to legal risk.

6) They fail to follow the steps of Matthew 18 or 1 Corinthians 5, depending on the circumstance. In a Matthew 18 situation, for instance, they fail to begin the process by confronting sin privately.

7) They misjudge how quickly to move toward formal discipline, either by dragging their feet or by rushing into judgment.

8) They fail to adequately teach and explain to a congregation why a particular act of discipline is necessary.

9) They tell the congregation too many details about a particular sin for which they are recommending discipline, embarrassing family members and causing weaker sheep to stumble.

10) They treat the processes of church discipline entirely as a legal process with little consideration for shepherding the unrepentant individual's heart.

11) They give little attention to the differences between *kinds* of sinners and how that might affect how long a church should bear with a pattern of sin before proceeding to subsequent stages of discipline (see 1 Thess. 5:14).

12) They forget that they too live by the gospel's provision of mercy, and therefore prosecute the discipline from a posture of self-righteousness. Other mistakes follow from this wrong posture, such as an overly severe tone and standoffishness.

13) They fail to truly love the sinner . . . by not begging the Lord for his or her repentance.

14) They demand too much from a smoldering wick or bruised reed. In other words, their stipulations for repentance are too high for someone who has been deeply enslaved in sin's grip.

15) They fail to properly instruct the congregation on how to interact with the unrepentant sinner, such as how to relate to him or her in social situations and how to pursue his or her repentance.

16) They fail to invite the disciplined individual to continue attending services of the church so that he or she might continue to hear God's Word (assuming there is no threat of criminal harm). Also, they fail to inform the church that everyone should hope for the disciplined individual to continue attending.

17) They put the responsibility for leading the discipline process entirely on the shoulders of one man, the senior pastor, thereby tempting individuals in the church to accuse the senior pastor of being personally vindictive.

18) They fail to have sufficient elder involvement in the congregation's life, such that the elders are unaware of the state of the sheep. This failure of formative discipline will inevitably weaken the church's ability to do corrective discipline well.

19) They fail to teach God's Word on a weekly basis.

20) They allow the congregation to approach a case of discipline with a wrongful spirit of retribution, rather than with the loving desire to warn the unrepentant sinner about God's ultimate retribution to come.

21) They pursue discipline on nonbiblical grounds (playing cards, dancing, etc.).

22) They pursue discipline for any reason other than for the good of the individual, the good of the church, the good of the onlooking community, and the glory of Christ.

SCRIPTURE INDEX

IX 9Marks

Building Healthy Churches

9Marks exists to equip church leaders with a biblical vision and practical resources for displaying God's glory to the nations through healthy churches.

To that end, we want to see churches characterized by these nine marks of health:

1 Expositional Preaching
2 Biblical Theology
3 A Biblical Understanding of the Gospel
4 A Biblical Understanding of Conversion
5 A Biblical Understanding of Evangelism
6 Biblical Church Membership
7 Biblical Church Discipline
8 Biblical Discipleship
9 Biblical Church Leadership

Find all our Crossway titles
and other resources at
www.9Marks.org